The Gift *of* You

HOW TO TELL YOUR LOVED ONES WHO YOU REALLY ARE

Dr. Bill McCord

CHICAGO
REVIEW
PRESS

Library of Congress Cataloging-in-Publication Data
Is available from the Library of Congress.

This book is dedicated to the people who
mean the most to me:
my wife and best friend, Amy,
and
our four sons, Eamon, Seth, Conor,
and Thomas.

© 2004 by Dr. Bill McCord
First edition
Published by Chicago Review Press, Incorporated
814 North Franklin Street
Chicago, Illinois 60610
ISBN 1-55652-535-4
Printed in the United States of America
5 4 3 2 1

"A straightforward way to improve communication with your loved ones. Written with insight and clarity."

—Eli Wallach, actor

"A wonderful, plain-talking book. It made me realize how much of my life I had never shared with my loved ones. I intend to put its suggestions to work immediately in my communications with my loved ones."

—Phyllis Diller, comedian

"A great book! I lent it to a friend who liked it so much, she read it twice!"

—Maureen Stapleton, Academy Award–winning actor

"*The Gift of You* is the best, simplest 'how-to' book ever; and maybe the most important. It shows you how to bridge the generation gap with love and honesty. It makes you wonder, 'Why didn't I think of that before?' If you don't think you need this book—you need it all the more. Thank you, Dr. McCord."

—Joseph Campanella, actor

"This is a must-read for everyone who wants to be more connected with the people they love the most. It boils down the essence of a loving relationship to the ability of loved ones to communicate honestly and openly with each other. A beautiful message in its simplicity and directness."

—Nanette Fabray, actor

"*The Gift of You* should be required reading in schools. It just makes sense. I loved this book!"

—Dick Martin, host of *Laugh-In*

"All in all, a nice little book to forge those most important of all connections—family ties. I was especially taken by the idea of using the phrase 'I love you' too readily in everyday life. After reading *The Gift of You*, I plan from now on to tell my loved ones just why I love them whenever I use that special phrase."

—Edward Asner, actor

"What a powerful message!"

—Alan Arkin, actor

"Your book is a great reminder for us all about what's important in life. We can all learn a lot from it."

—Dick Van Patten, actor

"I enjoyed reading *The Gift of You*. I found it to be insightful and moving."

—Stacy Keach, actor

"I can't tell you how much of my life I found in the pages of this book. My father left for the office at 7:30, returned at 5:45 to eat dinner promptly at 6:00 and then took a nap on the couch in the living room. He awakened as my brother and I went to bed. So much for bonding. Your book reminded me that it was time to let everyone know my feelings instead of assuming that they knew. All of us should understand the need to communicate our feelings. Thank you for putting it on paper."   —Arte Johnson, comedian

Contents

Acknowledgments

I want to thank Wayne Marshall of Danville, Kentucky, for helping me develop the "What and Why" concept for this book. Wayne has an uncanny ability to boil down complex and ambiguous ideas into their simplest and most compelling form. Without Wayne's help, this book would still be nothing more than an idea.

Thanks also to Dr. Robert Bogdan, Dual Professor of Cultural Foundations in Education and Sociology at Syracuse University, for teaching me the interviewing skills I used with the more than two hundred people who shared their lives and memories with me for this book.

And thank you to all of those same people who helped bring my simple ideas to life. Without their strength of character and willingness to become vulnerable, this book would have been only a skeleton—the bones of "I love you" without the flesh of "This is Why."

The following publisher has generously given permission to use the quotation on pages 187–88 of Chapter 10: from *The O'Reilly Factor: The Good, the Bad, and the Completely*

❧ Acknowledgments ❧

Ridiculous in American Life by Bill O'Reilly, copyright 2002 by Broadway Books.

I also gratefully acknowledge the overwhelming response of the celebrities and authors who have endorsed the book. Their praise adds credibility to a very simple concept; the author is humbled by their willingness to become part of the What and Why of his life.

Foreword

by Bernie Siegel, M.D.

Bestselling author of *Love, Medicine & Miracles* and
Prescriptions for Living

I know from personal experience how much I have learned about myself, my parents, and my family from their stories. If not for stories, I would not know why we are the people we are today, and why we act as we do. I was born an ugly duckling whom my parents hid from the neighbors. If I had not heard the story of my birth and how my grandmother accepted and loved me, I would never understand who I am today. The same is true for stories about my parents as well.

Helen Keller said it best: "Deafness is darker by far than blindness." We are separated from people when we do not listen to each other's feelings, experiences, and stories. As author Isabel Allende said, "There is only one thing truer than the truth, a story."

Again from personal experience, I know how stories affect even the most intellectual of audiences, who argue over statistical validity when presented with research findings, but who listen intently when they are told a story, anecdote, or case history.

Dialogue makes us one and gives us the gift of each other. Stories tell us about feelings that originate in the heart, while statistics and facts come from our heads and only relate to what we think. The heart is where the truth is stored, within your treasure chest. I hope that by reading *The Gift of You*, you will find it easier to open your treasure chest and share the richness of your life stories with the people who mean the most to you.

Author's Foreword

"Do you think he loved me?"
I told her, "I honestly do."
And then she said, "In all the years we were
married, he never told me he did."

John's elderly mother whispered these sad words to him while they knelt together beside her husband's casket. Forty-eight years of marriage had come to an end, and she was left wondering aloud if her husband really loved her. John recalled that when it came to what his father thought about his life or how he felt about his family, "You had to figure those things out on your own . . . because a lot was left unsaid."

I hope this book gives you the help and encouragement to tell your loved ones the things you need to say to them. John's father might have assumed his wife and son knew he loved them. Perhaps he thought thirty-five years of sweat and toil at the same job proved how much he loved them. But they were never sure. Now he is gone, and they are left wondering about his feelings for them. After all those years of living together, they still aren't convinced he loved them. If he did, they will never know.

Don't leave your loved ones struggling to understand who you really are and what you think about them. The pathway to showing them how much they mean to you is a simple one. Tell them the What and Why of your life! When you tell them the What of your life, you let them know what matters to you; what your greatest hopes are, what worries you, what gives you comfort and inspiration. They will know what makes you get out of bed every morning, fight the traffic, work as hard as you do, return home, and start over again the next day.

And when you tell them the Why of your life, you help them understand why you live your life the way you do. Why you are an accountant, teacher, or truck driver. Why you go to church on Sundays. Why you plant a garden in the backyard every year. Why you check on your elderly neighbor after work or why you talk to your favorite sister on the phone every Saturday night.

It's important to say, "I love you." But when you share a What or a Why, you put meat on the bones of every "I love you." You clearly express to your loved ones that you value them so much, you are even willing to let them know who you are by telling them what you are thinking about! One freely given What or Why can be worth a thousand "I love you's." A lifetime of the What and Why of your life is a priceless legacy to the people you love, more valuable than all the money and possessions you could possibly leave them.

Introduction

I originally envisioned this project as a book on estate planning. I spent thirteen years as a financial planner. As my clients aged, our attention naturally turned toward the best ways of passing their assets on to children and grandchildren. I, like most other financial planners, attorneys, and accountants who work with older people, urged my clients to plan for the disposition of their money and possessions. Proper estate planning makes good sense.

But after years of exhorting my clients to make a will, establish a trust, get nursing-home insurance, or write a Letter of Last Instructions, I began to realize that no one ever showed any excitement or satisfaction at the prospect of someday leaving a pile of money to his or her family. In fact, most people preferred to postpone any discussion of estate planning for as long as they possibly could. Their discomfort didn't seem to stem from a reluctance to face their own mortality. Most talked openly, honestly, and rather matter-of-factly about old age, infirmity, and the inevitability of their own deaths.

After reflecting on those hundreds of estate-planning meetings with clients and after listening to the older people I interviewed for this book, I discovered that in the home-stretch of life we are much more likely to measure the significance of our lives and our legacy not by the size of the bank account we will leave behind or by the complexity of our estate plan, but by the success we have had instilling in our loved ones values such as honesty, integrity, hard work, and a family-first attitude. The same people who seemed reluctant, indifferent, or sometimes annoyed at spending even a few minutes talking about the dispersal of their assets after death would gladly spend hours telling me stories about their children and grandchildren!

I'll never forget my meeting with Lydia, a longtime client. She was bringing me copies of her estate documents. She had just received them in the mail from her attorney. I asked her if, after reviewing them, they accurately reflected how she wanted her assets dispersed to her family. She smiled at me and said, "Oh, I think so. I can't make any sense out of all those legal papers. Look, I did it to please my kids. They feel like they did their duty getting me to the lawyer. I know they mean well. And I know you do too. Now we can stop talking about it. It's done. There are a lot more important things in life to talk about—like my two grandsons. Now those two are worth talking about!"

The more I worked on my estate-planning book, the more I thought about that conversation with Lydia and similar conversations with many of my other clients. So I decided to change direction. After a series of extensive interviews, what began as a book to describe the best ways to transfer your wealth upon death ended up as a book about giving your loved ones a much more important gift—the living legacy of you.

A friend of mine who grew up in rural Kentucky likes to filter the comings and goings of everyday life through this bit of country wisdom: "It doesn't take all day to look at a horseshoe." It's his way of pointing out the human propensity to turn simple truths into tortuously complex and convoluted arguments. I tried to keep his advice in mind as I wrote this book. The truth I hope you recognize and act upon is as straightforward as examining a horseshoe—you are your loved ones' most precious legacy. It's as simple as that!

By listening to the people in this book, you can recognize this simple truth and begin to consciously pass on the legacy of you to those who are waiting to hear it. My mother and father are both dead. I, like so many people who will speak to you in this book, am left looking at life with my parents through a rearview mirror distorted by a lack of meaningful communication and the passage of time.

Your legacy can and should be a better one. Going forward from here, you can give your loved ones their legacy—the gift of you—now and for as long as you are with them. As you become more comfortable sharing your life openly and spontaneously, you'll not only give your most valuable asset to the people you love, you'll also experience richer and more meaningful relationships with them.

Dr. Bill McCord
Colorado Springs, Colorado

I

The Ladder of Separation

Four years after I graduated from college, my mother phoned to tell me that Dad had been rushed to the hospital. He had rarely been sick with even a cold until he was diagnosed with advanced colon cancer. He died several months later.

Twenty-six years have passed since we buried my dad. As I grow older, I think more about my father and deeply regret that, although we lived together in the same house for so many years, I never really knew him. I do know he was the hardest-working man I had ever seen. He climbed telephone poles and repaired lines for Bell Telephone Company for forty-two years. I don't think he missed even one day of work at Ma Bell. Five days a week, he walked the same seven blocks to the telephone garage, carrying his black lunch pail and smoking a five-cent

White Owl cigar. When he returned home at the end of the day, he usually headed down the basement stairs to his workshop. He came up to the kitchen each night at 5:45 to eat the dinner my mother had prepared for us. Then, he went back down to the basement, working many nights long after my brother, four sisters, and I had gone to bed.

The true measure of my father's devotion to work was the annual ritual of scraping and repainting our house. When someone asks, "What was your father like?" I see him on a blistering hot August day standing near the top of a paint-stained wooden ladder with a cigar firmly planted in his mouth, a putty knife in one hand, and a small acetylene torch in the other. As he worked his way across each side of our two-story wooden frame house from top to bottom, he meticulously burned and scraped off every speck of paint. It seemed like he only came down to eat lunch or occasionally to find me. He would need me to steady the ladder as he climbed to the top rung in order to burn and scrape under the eaves of the house. I would brace my body against the ladder, flecks of paint falling in my hair, never uttering a word or even daring to look up at him, for fear that I might distract him and cause him to fall. Neighbors watched in amazement as my father, seemingly oblivious to everyone below, stood perched on his ladder for hours at a time in the sweltering heat and humidity of an upstate New York summer day, burning, scraping, and repainting with a patience even the saints would envy. He dedicated at least one week of his vacation, and sometimes both, to a task that today would probably be considered too cruel and unusual to inflict on a prison chain gang. No job was too hard for my dad. He kept on working until the last months of his life, when the cancer overcame him.

So, I immediately identified with the story of Dan Miller, a fifty-year-old accountant I interviewed for this book. I asked Dan what legacy he received from his father. Here is what he said:

My dad taught me how to work. He taught me the value of work. Life was not a lot of fun for him. He tried to earn a living and he worked hard at it. He was an insurance salesman. A lot of times he'd leave Monday morning to cover his territory and wouldn't come back until Friday. When he worked in town, he would work all day, come home at night, and we would eat at 5:30—not 5:00 or 5:15—exactly at 5:30. And then, at about 6:00, he would go back out and collect more insurance premiums from his customers. That was a big part of his life I had nothing to do with. I think it was tough for him when he retired because he lost his sense of worth. Nobody needed him. Nobody was asking for his advice.

Nobody was asking for his time. He didn't have any hobbies to fall back on. Work was his life.

Later in the interview, Dan remembered this:

My dad didn't say a lot. There really wasn't a lot of communication between us. I kind of knew my father cared for me because who else would go out and work as hard as he did to provide for me? And I think he felt I knew that, or at least thought I should.

Looking back at life with my father, I too "kind of knew" my dad cared about me. But like Dan's dad, mine didn't say much either. He never told me why he was up on that ladder summer after summer, burning and scraping and painting away the time we could have had for a family vacation. I know what my dad did—he worked hard almost all of the time—but I don't know why he did it.

Both Dan and I have backed into a scenario that reflects the way we hope things really were. We want to believe our fathers cared about us. But, in reality, we just aren't sure. I think my dad probably assumed I knew why he worked so hard. But I didn't know, and I still don't. He never talked with me about his life. Not about his work. Not about his family. Not about his feelings toward me. Our relationship could have been so much more meaningful if he would have come down the ladder just once to tell me why his life seemed to center around solitary work. Did he work so hard because he believed that's what a good father was supposed to do? Did he hope to set an example for us by working so hard? Was he in the basement or up on his ladder so much of the time for our welfare? Or did he want to avoid being with us? He never told me, and I will wonder why for the rest of my life.

The legacy I so desperately wanted from him, I never got. It wasn't his money or possessions that I wanted. I longed for him to tell me what mattered to him and why he lived his life the way he did.

After a year of interviewing more than two hundred people from all parts of the United States, I found that most had lived with their own version of parents standing on ladders. I talked to people who grew up on farms in Kansas, Nebraska, and Oklahoma during the Depression and the Dust Bowl. I talked with Japanese-Americans relocated to internment camps during World War II and to baby boomers and Generation Xers raised in New York City, Los Angeles, Chicago, and Dallas.

I talked with people from all walks of life, including active and retired accountants, postal workers, real-estate developers, stockbrokers, teachers, and homemakers, ranging in age from thirty-five to eighty-three. Most had children, but some did not. People reached back into their lives and tried to articulate what mattered to their parents and why they lived their lives the way they did. But like Dan Miller and me, most of the people I interviewed for this book aren't sure either. Most ate dinner every night with their mothers and fathers and lived with them under the same roof for years, but to this day they continue to wonder what their parents were thinking about and how they felt about them. They were never told.

Don't assume your loved ones understand the What and Why of your life because they live with you. I lived in the same house with my dad for the first eighteen years of my life. If working hard, which I saw him do every day, was part of the legacy he wanted to give me, he didn't say so. My dad's legacy to me will always be incomplete, because I don't know what, if anything, he wanted me to learn from his life!

It's the same for Dan Miller and scores of other people who will talk to you in this book. They can describe how their parents conducted their lives because those are the things they saw and lived with day after day. But most struggle mightily to explain what mattered to their parents or why they lived their lives the way they did. Sixty-, seventy-, and eighty-year-old people are still wondering who their parents really were. They lived together all those years without their parents telling them, even once, the What and Why of their lives.

Children grow old and die without really knowing the people who brought them into this world and raised them to adulthood. Nothing can replace this lost legacy. Not all the money and possessions you leave them in your Last Will and Testament. Not even a twenty-page autobiography or a thirty-minute videotape of yourself, with instructions to read or view in the event of your death. Nothing can replace giving yourself to the people you love while you live your lives together.

If you are on track to leave a legacy of silence, start changing direction right now. Through small and seemingly insignificant interactions, you can consciously and purposefully give your legacy to the people you love. Here's an example. I frequently travel on work-related business. I initiated an unspoken tradition with my ten-year-old son, Thomas. Each time I return home from a trip, I give Thomas an inexpensive gift, usually the latest Lego toy or a model car. At first, I eagerly anticipated giving him the gift and watching his face light up as he opened it. But the thrill was quickly gone for both of us.

It wasn't long before I was procrastinating until the last minute and hurriedly finding something for him in one of the airport gift shops. I even began asking my wife to buy something for me to give to Thomas! Bringing home that gift had become an annoyance to me. In turn, my son seemed increasingly disinterested or disappointed in whatever I gave him. Soon we were just going through the motions. The gift didn't seem to matter to either of us anymore.

The night before a flight home from New York City, I was watching TV in my hotel room when my thoughts turned to Thomas and the gift I would be giving him the next day. I realized that I never told Thomas why I gave him a gift each time I returned home. In fact, I was not clear in my own mind why I gave him a gift. I turned off the TV and spent a few minutes wrestling with the reasons I had started giving Thomas a gift in the first place, and why it had lost its excitement for both of us.

The next day, I was once again eager to give my son his gift. This time I not only had something to give to Thomas, I also had something important to tell him. After he opened his gift, I asked, "Thomas, do you know why I give you something each time I come home from a trip?" He thought for a few seconds and replied, "No, Dad, I don't." I said, "I give you a gift because it lets me show you that I am thinking about you and miss you when I am away and that I am so happy to see you when I get back home." Thomas replied, "Oh, that's nice, Dad." Then I told him, "Sometimes I probably give you just what you want and other times I don't. But every gift I give you is a way for me to say to you one more time, 'I love you very much.'" Thomas smiled and said, "Thanks, Dad . . . Can I put this together now?" Then he found the glue and paint and went to work assembling the model Ford truck I had just given him.

Did my twenty-second discussion with Thomas have an impact on him? I don't know. I may never know. But it did make me feel like I had moved another step down my ladder closer to Thomas by telling him what he meant to me and why I wanted to keep alive the budding tradition of giving him a gift. This simple ritual of giving a gift provided me with a perfect opportunity to tell my son a small part of the What and Why of my life.

Where We Are Headed

In Chapter 2 of this book, you will hear the same message from three generations: sharing the meaning of our lives with those we love, especially when we are raising them, usually takes a backseat to simply getting through the rigors and rituals of everyday life. But as the older people in this book warn, the regrets mount as time passes. Parents grow old. Children move away. People approach the end of their lives wishing they had shared more about themselves with their loved ones, especially when their children were young. You will discover that each generation creates its own ladder of separation and has its own reasons for doing so. For example, people who grew up during the Great Depression, Dust Bowl, and World War II hypothesized that their emotionally distant parents were, as one seventy-three-year-old woman told me, "too busy trying to survive to worry about the self-esteem of their children."

Many of these children of hard times said that when they became parents, they were so busy working and raising their families, they never had a chance to talk with their loved ones about the What and Why of their lives. Now, their thirty-five- to forty-year-old children explain that they are too busy and their kids are too young to listen to their own thoughts on life and legacy. They intend to talk about it "later on." Will they? Their grandparents didn't. Neither did their parents. And now they are repeating the behavior of past generations.

I think my father stood on his ladder for so many years that, even if he'd recognized the distance he put between himself and his family, he wouldn't have known how to take that first step toward us. How would he have begun talking to us about himself after a lifetime of silence? There was no one to show him. But as you read this book, you'll learn how.

Chapter 3 offers you a simple way to determine if you are standing on your own ladder. If you think you are, you'll find out how to come back down, one rung at a time.

The next three chapters give you a simple way to turn the ordinary events of everyday life—the What and Why—into a purposeful legacy for the people you love. In Chapter 4, you'll learn to clarify what matters in your life: for example, what your favorite grandmother really meant to you, what your job means to you, or what you hope to accomplish during the next ten years of your life. Chapter 5 shows you how to clarify why you live the way you do: why you teach elementary school, why you volunteer at the local soup kitchen, or why you coach your son's baseball team. You will be able to talk about why you still attend church, even though you complain about it every Sunday morning! Chapter 6 explains how to deliver the What and Why of your life out loud and face-to-face with the people you love.

Chapter 7 urges you to remember that it's your legacy to give. You, not the people around you, determine what it is. You'll hear from a man who struggles to define his own legacy, while his son constantly tells him it's all about money! Chapter 8 will explore how dramatically relationships can improve when sharing your What and Why becomes an everyday part of life for you.

As you read further, you may begin thinking not only about how to share the What and Why of your life with others, but also how you can ask those you love to begin sharing their lives with you. Chapter 9 will give you a strategy for asking them to start talking about themselves.

Chapter 10 sends you on your way with this thought: bringing the shortcomings of past family life out into the open in order to learn from them does not mean you are blaming others for your problems or indicting the parents you love so much. It can be the first step in a wonderful new beginning. It can lay the foundation for meaningful family communication that grows stronger with the passage of time. Your willingness to examine the good and bad of your life and share it with those you love—or to ask your loved ones to share their lives with you—can spark an intimate dialogue and emotional closeness that can define the way your family interacts for generations to come!

2

Living and Giving Consciously

Too Focused on Living

Life can get in the way of living. We have so much to do each day, it's hard to find time to think about where we are headed. This seems to be especially true for parents raising children. Maxine, a seventy-year-old mother and grand-mother, remembered:

> When we were young, Bob was working every day to make a living and meet his responsibilities, and I was taking care of the children. We had neither the time nor the awareness to think about our relationship with the kids. We were just too focused on living.

Everyone I interviewed felt that building strong relationships with their loved ones was a matter of the utmost importance. Everyone also agreed that the building process should occur at the front-end of raising children, not after they are grown and gone. But no one had consciously done it that way. Why? For the same reason Maxine gave. We are too focused on living!

Parents in the 1920s and 1930s were busy surviving the Great Depression and the Dust Bowl. The "good old days," as one child of the Depression remembered, were not so good. They meant finding enough food to eat and enough coal to heat the house. In the 1940s, people were busy fighting a world war. After the war, parents were busy building a better life for their children. As the son of a World War II veteran recalled, "My father was a doctor. He had no choice whether he wanted to be a doctor or a father. The two were not compatible at that time. What was expected of men was simply to provide, and he did a great job of providing."

Today's parents are busier than ever building a comfortable life for their children. A thirty-seven-year-old construction worker said he and his wife "want our kids to have every advantage." Consequently, they are working at full throttle to build a college fund for their three children, transport them to hockey camp, ballet, and soccer, and send them to the best private schools.

Our grandparents were too busy surviving the Depression. Our fathers were too busy being the providers and our mothers being the homemakers in post–World War II America. Now, we are too busy trying to accumulate a level of wealth, comfort, and opportunity for our families that would have been beyond our parents' and grandparents' wildest dreams.

So, as the reasons for our busy lives change from one generation to the next, one thing remains constant: we are so busy living, we have little or no time to think about life. Consequently, we tend to overlook the opportunities to tell our loved ones the What and Why of our lives at the precise time it would have the greatest impact on them—when they are young, malleable, and eager to learn!

And Then It's Too Late

It's a lot easier to think about what you want your legacy to be when you are older. Your kids are grown, and you have time to think about it.

Ginny, sixty-four years old and the mother of four grown children, shook her head as she told me that it's much easier to think about your legacy after the children are grown and gone than it is while you are raising them. But by then, as Ginny said, you are no longer thinking of creating a legacy. You are simply hoping that you left the right one. You are also looking for evidence in the lives of your grown children that your legacy was a good one.

Like almost all of the people I interviewed, you will probably hope you left your children a legacy of honesty, integrity, hard work, being a loving parent and spouse, and other life-enhancing values. But you might also find yourself feeling like Darlene, a sixty-eight-year-old retired telephone worker and mother of four children, who said, "I realize now that I never really thought about it at all. A lot of time goes by and then it's too late."

Most people in their sixties and seventies said they couldn't think about a legacy until they "had the time and money to finally relax," as Norman put it. But even then, he admitted not giving it much thought, if any at all. It was the same for virtually all of the retirees I interviewed. Yes, they now had time to think about it; but no, they still had not quite gotten around to it! It may be easier to think about your legacy when you are older and your family is grown and gone, but it is not more likely that you really will.

If you didn't talk about yourself when you lived together, you probably won't start when your children are adults and living on their own. You will continue to interact with them in much the same way as you did when you raised them. As Joe, a successful real-estate developer, reminded me regarding my relationship with my ten-year-old son, "If you wait to think about it until you are in your sixties, how are you going to approach Thomas when he is thirty and say, 'This is what I think is important in life and what I want for you'?" Joe's right. It will be much more difficult for me to approach Thomas when he is grown and gone. I need to start right now, so he and I have years to learn how to talk and listen to each other about the stories that constitute our lives.

Not Everybody Gets That Lucky

My dad was very sick. He called a family meeting. All my brothers and sisters were in the room, all nine of us. He talked about his will and where he wanted his property to go, that kind of thing. That sort of opened the door for him. When you start talking about those kinds of things, then I guess the other things are not as hard to talk about. After he talked about his financial assets, he started talking about his memories of childhood and what was important to him and what he wanted to pass on to us and to his grandchildren. Because he was busy working, he did not have the time for us, the way he did for the grandkids. He ran a hardware store in town and he had to be there every day. On Sundays he went in to do the books and stock the shelves. He said how much he wished he would have had more time for us kids. He told each of us how much we meant to him. I never heard him talk like that before. So, I guess I was really fortunate my father opened up like that. Not everybody gets that lucky.

At death's door, Nancy's seventy-five-year-old father started talking about his life. He was finally able to tell his adult children what was important to him and how much he loved them. A few weeks later, he died. Nancy, forty-two years old at the time, felt lucky. She got to hear her father "open up," as she called it. She was lucky compared to many of us who watch our parents go silently to their graves. She was lucky because she squeezed out a few minutes of meaningful communication with her father just before he died.

Marie, a forty-year-old social worker, remembers the day her grandfather gathered the grandchildren around his deathbed so he could "tell us more about his life." Marie paused at the end of her story and said, "I guess you don't think about it until you know you are not going to live much longer."

That's the way it happens for so many of us. We could live a hundred years without spending five minutes telling our loved ones who we are. Then, if we linger long enough at the end and still have our mental capacities, we might open up to them in the last hours or minutes of our lives, like Nancy's father and Marie's grandfather did.

How do we live more purposefully than this? How do we better negotiate the demands of this turbo-charged world that steal so much of our time and energy? How do we make sure that we have not left the essence of our time together buried under a pile of life's activities and that we will not be saying exactly what our parents and grandparents said throughout the interviews: "I wish I would have spent more time with my kids"? How do we make sure that our children aren't left considering themselves "lucky" because only on our deathbeds did we finally gave them a taste of the intimacy they longed for all the years we lived together?

It Takes Only a Few Minutes

My kids and grandkids are always saying "I love you" to each other. We didn't do that when they were growing up. It's nice to hear—although they say it so much, sometimes I wonder how much meaning it really has.

Diane marvels at how easily and freely her children and grandchildren tell each other, "I love you." She rarely said it to her children. Her parents never said it. She doesn't remember anyone in her generation dispensing "I love you's" as matter-of-factly as younger people today seem to do. But she's also a little suspicious about it. They say it so often, she questions how much meaning and sincerity the words really have.

Just being able to say "I love you" with such ease and freedom is a wonderful characteristic of today's younger parents. But how do we give depth to the words? How do we keep "I love you" from becoming little more than a substitute for such pleasantries as "Have a nice day"?

Here's one way. Occasionally, finish an "I love you" with a What or a Why from your life. Instead of telling your son, "I love you," and leaving it at that, you might say, "I love you, and I want to tell you why. I love you so much because. . . ." You complete the sentence. You add the power and meaning to each "I love you"!

Most of us would like to slow down, work less, and spend more time with the people we love. But we might never do it. We live in a world that moves faster every day and demands that we keep pace. It's a world of stress and fatigue with both parents working, expensive car and mortgage payments, day-care costs, and a seemingly endless number of after-school activities that we shuttle our kids to and from. That's life! We have learned to adapt by living on the fly. We have even learned to say "I love you" on the fly. Now, we need to learn how to give our loved ones the What and Why on the fly.

Here's an example. You have ten minutes in the car with your sixth-grade daughter. It's another Wednesday afternoon. You are rushing her to soccer practice. Instead of wasting the time complaining that you'll be late for your four o'clock business meeting, give your daughter a taste of the Why of your life. Tell her why it's important to you to take time out of your jam-packed Wednesdays to drive her to practice. Tell her why it's important to *you* that she plays soccer after school. Not why it's important to her. You have probably told her that a hundred times, and she doesn't need to hear it again. This time, tell her why it is important to *you*.

By telling her that, you are letting her into your world. Maybe your daughter playing soccer matters to you because you didn't get a chance to participate in organized sports when you were her age. Instead, you had a newspaper route or babysat to earn money. Maybe you felt left out because you didn't play any team sports and missed the chance to pursue your athletic talents. If that's the case, tell her. When you do, you let her know a little bit more about your life and how much she means to you. In effect, you are giving a powerful "I love you" to your daughter. Multiply this one instance by the number of times you have an opportunity to give her the What and Why on the fly. Before long, your legacy will take shape. Each time you share a little more of the What and Why, the next time is easier. You will find endless opportunities to build your legacy—on the way to school, at dinner, watching a TV show together, at the mall, anywhere and everywhere. For example, during a meal together, you might talk to your kids about what your job means to you. Or why you just changed jobs. During the morning drive to school, you may talk about one of your teachers who had a special interest in you or about why you felt so awkward and out of place in high school but discovered your self-confidence after you left home for college.

Whether or not your kids act interested at the time, they will remember each What and Why you give them, whether it relates to the most serious issues in your life or the most unimportant. Just tell them. It's one of the greatest gifts you will give them. It's probably what you wanted more of from your parents, what your parents wanted more of from your grandparents. You don't have to alter your lifestyle to tell them. If you want to eat a family meal at home each night and tell a story about yourself at the dining room table, that's great. But you can also do it while eating a Big Mac and fries at McDonald's. The setting doesn't matter; saying it does.

No Children, No Legacy?

For most of us, our children are the natural recipients of our legacy. But that's not true for everyone. I talked with several people who don't have children or who are much more emotionally connected to other family members than to their own offspring. For example, Natalie, a forty-five-year-old school psychologist, never married or had children. But she has a special bond with her niece Janet, a freshman at Brown University. Since Janet was a baby, Natalie has saved to pay her college expenses. She talks about Janet like a proud parent preens about a successful son or daughter. Natalie loves her niece as much as any parent could love a son or daughter.

I also talked with Emily, a widow and mother of two grown children. She admits that, for many reasons, she has never been particularly close to her two children. The loves of her life, at age seventy-three, are a five-year-old boy and a three-year-old girl. They are her grandchildren, Joey and Amanda. Emily lives in an apartment below her son, daughter-in-law, and precious grandchildren. Her eyes filled with tears when she said, "Those two kids bring me more joy than anyone could imagine."

If Natalie shares the What and Why of her life with anyone, it will probably be with Janet, her beloved niece. For Emily, it will be her grandchildren. For someone else, it might be a spouse, a favorite sister, a parent, or even a parent-in-law. Someone other than your own child might matter the most to you, and therefore be the likely recipient of your legacy.

The giving of your legacy might even extend to people outside of your family. Hazel Martin lived next door to my family for thirty-five years. She lived alone during most of that time. Hazel was a young woman when her husband, a police officer, was killed while attempting to make an arrest. Mrs. Martin, as we respectfully called her, had no children, and toward the end of her life, no living family. But her life was full of people who loved her. Mrs. Martin was a first-grade teacher for forty-seven years at the same school, P.S. 6 in Kingston, New York. She was truly an institution within an institution. She taught three generations from the same families—grandparents, parents, and grandchildren. Mrs. Martin had a constant stream of visitors to her house. Most were pupils from many years ago who faithfully kept in touch with her over the years. She always had twenty or thirty new cards and letters of thanks from her former students taped to the wall above her living-room fireplace.

This frail, little old lady touched the lives of hundreds of people during her lifetime. She had no children or other family to give her legacy to. She gave it all—her wisdom, caring, and thoughts about life—to the thousand plus children who were fortunate enough to have her as their first-grade teacher. Like

Mrs. Martin, countless teachers, physicians, nurses, counselors, and others have had a profound and lasting impact on the people they have cared for in the course of their everyday work.

So, you might have others beside family members to whom to give your legacy. They might include people from the community you have helped and guided over the years, friends, or perhaps coworkers. They might even include people you will never know! John Adams, the second president of the United States, wrote more than a thousand letters to his wife, Abigail, during the struggle for American independence. Historians believe his letters had a dual purpose. First of all, they were meant as a personal exchange between husband and wife. But they were also a vehicle for Mr. Adams to share his thoughts, struggles, and desires with friends and other family members. Mr. Adams expected them, in turn, to share the letters with their own friends and family. Adams's letters might have been America's first chain letters! Over two hundred years later, John Adams is still sharing the What and Why of his life with today's history students and others who read his personal letters.

Although this book, for purposes of simplicity, boils down the gift of you to its most common denominator—parents and children—you might have other people in mind. Sharing the What and Why of your life is one of the deepest and most personal expressions of your love for others, whoever they might be.

As you read this book, identify those people and how you and they might both benefit from the deeper intimacy that comes from a true sharing of your life—what matters to you and why you live life the way you do. You might not share your legacy on the grand scale that John Adams did and still does today, but even if you share it with only one person, start right now. Don't let that part of you quietly slip away. After all, it's who you are. It's what defines your life. It's your most precious gift to those you love. Give it without reservation or hesitation. Give it to those who mean the most to you, family and non-family alike!

❖   ❖   ❖

In the next chapter, you'll self-administer the "ladder test." It's a way for you to step back and gauge how much of the What and Why of your life you have already shared with your loved ones. It also gives you insight into how easy or difficult it might be for you to divulge personal and emotional matters to those you love. Taking the ladder test will set the stage for you to learn a simple way to identify what is important to you, why you live your life the way you do, and, of course, how to share both with the people you love.

3

Are You Standing on a Ladder?

The most striking similarity across the three generations of people I interviewed was the absence of parents sharing the What and Why of their lives with their children. From grandparents to parents to adult children who today are in their thirties and forties, the What and Why remain unspoken. Again, let's be clear about the What and Why we are discussing here. Many parents are able to tell their kids what they should do and why they should do it. In fact, most people see this as a fundamental duty of parenthood. *But virtually no one heard their parents say what was important to them or why they lived their lives like they did.*

Nor have they told their own children. If this includes you, begin sharing the What and Why of your life right now. It will only require a few simple changes in how you interact with your loved ones.

Start by self-administering the ladder test. It helps you gauge how successful you have been in sharing the stories of your life with your loved ones. You will answer three separate sets of questions. Each set corresponds to one of the three steps in the legacy-building approach you will learn in Chapters 4, 5, and 6.

What Matters to You?

I don't want my legacy to be measured in terms of the money I leave them. Is it Warren Buffett who is planning to give all his money away to charity? I like that. The people I know who have been left a large inheritance—who didn't earn the money—wasted it. I don't think it helped them to be better people. I think when you go out and earn it, you have more pride in yourself. My kids, of course, would probably die if they heard me say this but, really, I wouldn't want to deprive them of the feeling you have when you do well financially on your own. It's easy to give them too much.

Bob is a successful urologist and the father of three daughters ranging in age from late teens to mid-twenties. He agreed to meet with me at his office after his last appointment of the day. When I arrived, he reminded me that he only had twenty minutes to talk because this was his afternoon to catch up on paperwork. Two hours later he was still leaning forward in his chair, smiling and telling me stories about what it was like to run a busy medical practice and raise three daughters at the same time. It was obvious that Bob loved his three girls.

But near the end of our conversation, Bob's smile was gone. He sat back in his chair and in a somber tone of voice told me that not only does he think his legacy is about more than his money and possessions, he believes that leaving a large monetary inheritance would not be in the best interests of his children. He strongly feels that when it involves your own children, "It's easy to give them too much." But he has not shared his feelings about this with his daughters, and he's not sure he ever will. Why wouldn't Bob tell them how he feels about something that seems to matter so much to him and will sooner or later matter to them? Here's the reason he gave: "I don't see why I should upset them by talking about something [his death and their inheritance] that hopefully won't happen until way down the road."

Think what might happen if Bob decides to give a sizable part of his wealth to charity upon his death, instead of to his daughters. Suppose he does so without ever telling them his reasons. He dies, his money goes to strangers, and his daughters never know why. Was he angry with them? Did he really think strangers deserved his assets more than his own children?

If he starts telling his daughters now that he thinks it's important for each of them to earn her own way through life, they won't be left bewildered and embittered after he dies, and most importantly, they'll learn more about how he views life. When he tells them, they might not like what they hear, but after his death they will clearly know why he did it.

The first part of giving the gift of you to your loved ones is to let them know what matters to you. When you do this, you make them privy to your hopes, dreams, failures, and successes. Some of what matters to you might be clearly visible to them and some of it might be a total mystery. Some of it you might have already accomplished and some of it you might still be trying to achieve. Some of it you might be proud of and some of it you might wish had never happened. What matters to you is usually laden with emotion. It's what you hold near and dear to your heart.

Here are three sets of "What" questions. As you read them, ask yourself which ones you have already thought about. Which ones have you discussed with your loved ones?

The Past

1. What people have had the most influence on your life?
2. What events have had the most influence on your life?
3. What memories of your childhood are most recurring?
4. What memories will you cherish the most?
5. What have been the high points in your life?
6. What have been the low points?
7. What would you have done differently in life?
8. What lessons have you learned from the past?

The Present

1. What matters the most to you?
2. What matters the least to you?

3. What are your greatest strengths?
4. What are your greatest weaknesses?
5. What would you like to change about your life right now?
6. What do you enjoy the most about your life?
7. What do you enjoy the most about each of your loved ones?
8. What do you consider to be the indicators of a successful life?

The Future

1. What do you still hope to accomplish in life?
2. What are your hopes for each of your loved ones?
3. What would a "perfect life" look like for you in five, ten, or fifteen years?
4. What would you like to be remembered for after you are gone?

Reread the list and identify the top three questions that you would like to use as a starting point in sharing the What of your life with your loved ones. In the next chapter, you'll try bringing one of the three questions down your ladder.

Why Do You Live the Way You Do?

When I was twenty-three, I was diagnosed with cancer. I had a four-year-old and a six-month-old. I figured if I died in the next few years, they had a good chance of not knowing who I was. You see, my dad died when I was only eight, and as best as I can remember, he was a very quiet person anyway. I really can't tell you one thing he said. And that was kind of rumbling around in my mind; that I wanted them to know who I was. I really didn't worry much about dying or what that whole experience would be like. I just kept thinking about my two kids growing up without me around and never knowing what I was like. So, I started to write each of them a letter explaining who I was. It was a kind of summary, I guess you'd call it, about what I liked to do and what was on my mind. Not what I thought about nuclear proliferation and stuff like that, but about the basic things in life. Why I liked sports and why I liked the outdoors. You know, the day-to-day things. I started to write all this down for them, but my medical situation took a turn for the better, so I never finished the letters.

The second part of giving the legacy of you to your loved ones is letting them know why you live your life the way you do. The Why of your life sheds light on your everyday behavior and thinking. At the age of twenty-three, Bill was unusually young to think about giving the Why of his life to his two children. But a battle with cancer gave him a heightened awareness of his own mortality and the resolve to make sure his children learned who he was. He knew that waiting until "later on" when his kids were older or he had more time might be too late. He might be gone before they even knew him. So he decided to write down the Why of his life. As he said, he wanted to make sure they learned about the Why of the "day-to-day things" in his life. But Bill's health improved and he stopped writing. The crisis was behind him. The sense of urgency was gone. When I asked him where the unfinished letters to his children are today, he told me that he really didn't know for sure, but he thought he probably threw them away.

What if you learn to treat the transfer of the Why of your life with the same seriousness and urgency that Bill did during those weeks and months when he thought he might die? And what if you learn to do this, not at the last minute when you think your life might be coming to an end, but as an ordinary part of yet another uneventful day? Your loved ones wouldn't be left wondering for the rest of their lives why you did or didn't do certain things. They'd know who you really are.

Here are three sets of "Why" questions. Why questions prompt you to let your loved ones know who you are by letting them see why you live life the way you do. Which of these Why questions have you discussed with your loved ones? After you read through the entire list, choose the three questions that you would like to use to begin a conversation with your loved ones about the Why of your life. In Chapter 5, you'll have an opportunity to bring one of the three questions down your ladder.

Relationships

1. Why did (didn't) I get married?
2. Why did (didn't) I have children?
3. Why did I get divorced?
4. Why do (don't) I enjoy meeting new people?
5. Why do I like one sibling more than another?
6. Why do (don't) I stay in touch with family back home and old friends from the past?
7. Why do (don't) I have a "best friend"?

Routine of Daily Life

1. Why do I work at my present job?
2. Why do (don't) I aspire to "work my way up" the job ladder?
3. Why do (don't) I save money?
4. Why have (haven't) I been financially successful?
5. Why do (don't) I enjoy solitary activities, such as reading or watching television?
6. Why do (don't) I like events with big crowds?
7. Why do (don't) I pursue hobbies?
8. Why do I read the newspaper each day by always starting with the sports/business/entertainment section?

Values/Religion/Politics

1. Why do (don't) I occasionally tell "little white lies?"
2. Why do (don't) I think it's okay to cheat a little on my income tax return?
3. Why do I obey some laws but not others?
4. Why do (don't) I attend church?
5. Why do (don't) I support the death penalty?
6. Why am I pro-choice or pro-life?
7. Why do (don't) I vote?
8. Why am I a political conservative, moderate, or liberal?

Can You Say It Out Loud?

> I never have talked to them [the children] about what went on in Vietnam. That is a personal thing . . . it was awful. To see young men—just boys, really—dead or with a hand or foot missing. I remember seeing the body bags stacked next to each other, waiting to go to the morgue. You can't realize what it's like if you haven't been there. I don't care how many film clips you see on television. It's just not the same.
>
> I know that it changed me forever. I came home a different person. And when I got home, it got worse. No one wanted to act like it even happened. Or if they mentioned it, they asked how I could participate in such an immoral war. It was an ugly war and everyone wanted to forget about it. Why should I dump that on my family? I don't want them to feel sorry for me. I have never shared my troubles with my family, even though they see my military medals and know they mean something. That is not something they need to know about. If they asked, I would probably share some of it. I think they know that.

Frank spent two tours of duty in Vietnam. He came back a decorated soldier from a war that he said "changed me for-ever." What he views as sharing his troubles with his family could be one of his best opportunities to tell them who he really is, by revealing his core values and beliefs. Why he risked his life. Why he volunteered to return to Vietnam for a second year. Why his time there changed his life. How it changed him. Frank's family should know about those two years of his life if he wants them to have a better understanding of who he really is. His legacy will be incomplete without sharing the What and Why of a part of his life that had such a profound and lasting impact on him. He's right. No one, including his family, can understand what happened by watching film footage of the war. He has to tell them. He told me, a stranger who really doesn't have to hear or understand it. It's his loved ones who need to hear him talk about it. They are the ones who need to know how this seminal event in his life shaped him as a husband and a father. For me, it's a touching story, but one that really doesn't belong to me. It belongs to his family. Frank's time in "the heat and hell" of Vietnam, as he called it, not only changed his life, but most likely, the lives of everyone in his family.

Often, the defining events of our lives are not as dramatic as Frank's, but they still have a profound effect not only on us but also on the lives of our loved ones. Ed is a sixty-year-old budget analyst for a national healthcare network. He spent

twenty years in the Air Force, working his way up to the rank
of Master Sergeant. Here's what happened next:

> I was on the list for promotion to Sergeant Major. That was
> my goal in the military. That, to me, was being the best you
> could be. My dad reached the rank of Sergeant Major. My
> dream was to do the same. And my time had finally arrived.
> But as much as I wanted it, I just couldn't do that to my
> family. It would have meant another overseas tour. We had
> moved around enough. Both girls were close to high-school
> age and they needed a stable place to live. It was a choice
> between my career or my family. I had to do what was right
> for them. So I gave up my career in the Air Force and we
> settled down in a nice neighborhood two blocks from the
> high school. I've got to tell you, it was one tough decision to
> make. But I had to make it. When all is said and done, family
> comes first.

Ed has never told his children or grandchildren why he
left the military. Do they know the personal sacrifice he
made because "family comes first?" He's not sure. This story
is a piece of Ed's legacy to his children. He can still give it

even at this late date, if he tells his family what he did and why he did it.

Don't let the What and Why of your life remain buried deep inside of you. First, bring them into the light so you can examine them. Then, deliver them to your loved ones. When you do, you risk exposing yourself to their disinterest, discomfort, or unwillingness to accept what you have to say. But regardless of how your loved ones react to them, these things still need to be said. If you leave them to chance, your loved ones might fail to recognize the What and Why of your life, or they might totally misinterpret them.

I heard countless stories from people who assumed that their actions clearly demonstrated what mattered to them, only to find out later that their loved ones understood little or nothing about what they had seen.

Jake and Ann, for example, spent a year living in St. Petersburg, Russia, doing volunteer work with an international organization. Jake knew he would jeopardize the success of his construction business that, after five years of fifteen-hour workdays, had finally begun to turn a profit. He and Ann spent months raising money to pay their expenses in Russia. When Jake looked back, he felt the year in St. Petersburg was a defining event in his life. Ann felt the same way. They both assumed their two adult sons surely must have understood how important this year was to them. However, when they returned home, Jake said both sons talked about it like "we went on a vacation." Jake and Ann were astonished at what they saw as both sons' lack of insight into their lives. They had taken for granted that their sons would intuitively understand the What and Why of their year in Russia. But they didn't understand; not at all. Not the months of fund-raising, not the visits to the lawyer to update their estate documents in case something happened to them overseas, not the late nights sitting at the kitchen table making sure Jake's business wouldn't go under while they were away, and, most surprising of all, not the weekly letters from Russia talking about the desperate plight of the people in St. Petersburg that they were there to help.

So, after they returned home and one of their sons casually asked, "How was it over there?" Jake and Ann decided to spend time with both boys telling their story from its beginning. They explained how they got the idea of going to Russia, how they spent months discussing the pros and cons of such a major commitment, why they were willing to risk the business Jake had worked so hard to build, and what they thought they would accomplish when they got there. Finally, after two years of planning and another year actually living their dream, they made sure they gave their two boys the What and Why of this incredible year of their lives.

You certainly offer the gift of yourself to your loved ones by your example or through personal sacrifices like those of Frank, Ed, Jake, and Ann. But you can only be certain the gift has been delivered by telling your loved ones what your actions meant to you. Saying it out loud won't assure that they understand, accept, or are even interested in what you are telling them—but it does guarantee delivery. Saying it out loud is your way to FedEx the gift of you to the people you love. Like the slogan says, it's your way of getting it there "when it absolutely, positively has to be there on time." Treat it with that much importance—like it absolutely, positively has to be said to your loved ones, right now!

The following ten questions measure your ability to say the What and Why of your life out loud. Answer each question as openly and honestly as you can. Give yourself two points for each "Always," one point for a "Sometimes," and no points for a "Never." Tally your total score and place that number in the box at the bottom of the questionnaire.

Questions	Always	Some-times	Never
1. I am able to talk openly with my loved ones about personal and/or emotional issues.			
2. I can tell my loved ones why something matters to me, not just why I think it should matter to them.			
3. If I tell my loved ones something personal, I am comfortable if they don't agree or don't seem to understand or be interested.			
4. When I tell my loved ones something personal, I am comfortable if they ask me questions about it.			

Questions	Always	Some-times	Never
5. I can tell my loved ones something personal, even if it seems to make them uncomfortable.			
6. I think it is important to tell my loved ones the What and Why of my life.			
7. I can identify at least one opportunity during the day when I could talk to my loved ones about the What and Why of my life.			
8. I tell my loved ones stories about my life.			

9. I tell the stories just as they happened, even if shading the truth would make them sound better.			
10. I can answer questions my loved ones ask about my life with complete candor.			

Total Score = _____

How Far Up the Ladder Are You?

Assume you are standing on the top rung of the ladder shown on the next page. Imagine your loved ones at the bottom of the ladder looking up at you. With each step down, you move closer to them. Each step you take lets them more clearly hear you and see who you really are.

Starting at the top rung of the ladder, use your Total Score from above to move down one rung for each point you gave yourself. For example, if your Total Score is eleven points, move eleven rungs down the ladder. The closer you move to the bottom of the ladder, the easier it is for you to share the What and Why of your life. If you remain at or near the top of the ladder, you probably have significant difficulty talking about yourself with your loved ones.

Put a mark on the rung where you are currently standing. This will give you a benchmark to refer back to as you share the What and Why with your loved ones.

Where Are You Standing?

start here

The next three chapters will give you the tools you need to move down your ladder. As you become more proficient in sharing the What and Why of your life, you can retake the ten-question test as often as you like and each time reposition yourself on the ladder. You'll be able to see how much progress you are making in your attempt to move closer to your loved ones. You'll immediately begin moving down your ladder as soon as you share the first What or Why with the people you care about the most.

4

Knowing What Matters to You

Discounted Lives

> I really don't know why you want to talk with me. As far as
> my legacy goes, I probably won't have much of anything to
> leave to my children.

An absolute prerequisite to sharing what matters to you
and why you live life the way you do is to first believe that the
What and Why of your life have enough value to give to the
people you love.

Let's look at Donna's life. She couldn't understand why I
wanted to talk with her. She barely scrapes by on a small pen-
sion and Social Security. She drives a dented, 1985 Chevrolet

with more than 150,000 miles on the odometer. She lives alone in a rickety house that hasn't been painted in years. We sat in her living room during our interview. She apologized that the chair I sat on needed to be reupholstered and that the table that held our coffee cups was darkened by stains and age. She repeatedly told me that she rarely had visitors, so "since it's just me, I don't really mind living with all this worn-out stuff." She let out an embarrassed laugh but clearly was uncomfortable allowing me see the dilapidated condition of her home and furnishings.

Donna thought she was unqualified to speak about her legacy because she doubted that she had one to give. After all, as she quietly told me, "I have a second mortgage on the house. All the things I own couldn't be worth much more than a few thousand dollars. By the time they [her kids] pay for burying me, there won't be much of anything left." She saw herself as "a poor farm girl from the Midwest who never did anything special."

Then she started to tell her story of her life. Donna, the second youngest of eight children, grew up on a farm in Kansas during the Dust Bowl. Her father worked the fields seven days a week, but couldn't make ends meet. Donna worked after school, as did all her brothers and sisters, in order to bring home money to buy food and pay the bills. When she was in the seventh grade, she started doing housework for a few wealthy families in the nearby town. She remembered the teacher ringing a large iron bell behind the school; this was the signal for the children to quickly gather their books and run home before the enormous reddish-brown clouds of swirling dirt engulfed the town. She remembered days when the blowing dirt that seemed to seep into every crack of their hundred-year-old farmhouse "was so thick on the kitchen floor and table, it was easier to move it with a shovel than a broom."

But Donna was a voracious reader as a child and a straight-A student in school. She graduated at the top of her high-school class and went on to college, a rarity for women in that time and place. She earned an elementary school teaching certificate and taught third and fourth graders for more than thirty years. While her husband fought in Europe during World War II, she continued teaching and raised their four children by herself. Today, Donna is a seventy-seven-year-old widow with failing health. She had never told anyone, including her children, this beautiful story of her incredible fortitude and perseverance until I coaxed it out of her. Why not? Because she was convinced "nobody wants to hear about that. It was a long time ago. That's all ancient history."

And there is Eleanor, a retired New York City teacher. It wasn't until the last few minutes of our meeting that Eleanor said, "Oh, maybe you would like to hear about my growing-up years in Germany." She told this remarkable story:

On the day of my tenth birthday, we fled from the Nazis. My mother was Jewish and my father was a Christian. My father was repeatedly told by local Nazi leaders to renounce my mother and me as non-Aryan, which would have saved him, but meant deportation to a concentration camp for both of us. I remember that the local Nazi official in charge of our precinct used to be a friend of our family. My father kept telling my mother that she couldn't trust him anymore. I remember my mother saying, "Oh, that's ridiculous. I taught Dieter to read when he was a little boy. He wouldn't hurt us." But my father knew differently. He used go to a neighbor's apartment late at night and listen to BBC radio from London with some of his friends. They would huddle together under a blanket, doing everything they could to make sure no one in the next apartment could hear the radio. It was illegal to listen to the BBC. They could have been arrested. So he knew that sooner or later, the Nazis would come for us.

Eleanor's dad took action. He arranged for the entire family, including Eleanor's aunt and uncle, to escape to the United States. They left behind their home and most of their belongings, taking only what "could fit in one large wooden trunk," as Eleanor remembered it. They sailed to the United States and settled in New York City. Eleanor, who spoke only German, learned English in the New York City public schools and went on to teach for thirty-six years in that same school system. She even taught for ten years in the elementary school where she learned to speak English!

I asked Eleanor if she had shared this amazing part of her life with Eric, her forty-year-old son. She paused for a few seconds and said, "I don't know. I think I may have told him parts of it." When I asked if she was concerned that Stephen, her beloved six-year-old grandson, might never know this story about her, she said, "Well, I never thought about it. I guess I should probably write it down for him. . . . I won't be around forever, will I?"

Bill has enjoyed a successful career in banking and investments. He grew up in poverty in Louisiana. He was eight years old when his father died suddenly and only fourteen when his mother died after battling cancer. He and his brother then lived with their grandmother, but only for eight months until she too died. Bill was a fifteen-year-old sophomore in high school, living with his eighteen-year-old brother in their deceased grandmother's house. As Bill said, "During my teenage years, I wasn't raised by anybody but me. My brother went to the local college and had his own friends. So I was on my own—an orphan at age fifteen. Because I raised myself, I probably have been more willing than most people to let my kids learn by making their own mistakes. That's pretty much how I learned and I guess I turned out okay."

But Bill had not told his three children this story. Nor had he told them that, with virtually no help from anyone, he finished high school, worked his way through college, and received a degree in economics from Louisiana State University. As far as he knew, they had no idea that when he was their age, he was living alone, raising himself, and about to put himself through college. Consequently, they are unaware of a critical part of his life that, as Bill remembers, shaped his thinking and directly affected how he has raised them.

Donna, Eleanor, and Bill each told stories of perseverance, personal achievement, and events that had had a major impact on their lives and ultimately the lives of their children. However, as was the case with many others I interviewed, they told their stories to me, not to the people who needed to hear them—their children and grandchildren.

They didn't view their stories as opportunities to give their loved ones a special glimpse into their lives. Instead, they each treated their story like old news—of no interest or relevance to anyone anymore.

Throughout our interviews, people dismissed the most essential stories of their lives as boring, irrelevant, and meaningless. They repeatedly apologized for not having anything important to say about themselves. After all, what had they really accomplished? None were famous athletes or movie stars. None were politicians in the public eye. Only a few were centers of influence outside of their own family and small circle of friends. They were just ordinary people. Perhaps that's why they had difficulty seeing their extraordinary personal accomplishments.

Look at what they had really done. Some had survived the Dust Bowl and the Great Depression. Others had fought in world wars. Some had overcome the childhood trauma of living through the death of one or both parents. Most tirelessly worked to provide for their families. Almost all matter-of-factly told stories of self-sacrifice and self-denial in order to give their loved ones advantages they never had.

These are the kinds of lives most of us lead. They are the same quiet lives led by our friends and neighbors. They are not the kind of lives that make newspaper or television headlines. When we view them as ordinary and uninteresting, we tend to discount their importance and assume they are irrelevant to others.

A Shallow Legacy

When you get to be my age, you realize that what some people have been telling you for the last thirty or forty years might be true. Money may be a way of keeping score, but you may be playing the wrong game.

When I asked what came to mind when people heard the word "legacy," most said money. But when I asked if money was the most important part of their legacies, everyone, from the poorest to the richest, said no.

Peter, a college professor nearing retirement, summed up the thoughts of most people when he said, "If my wife and I have any money left when we die, we want the kids to have it. But if it were strictly about money, it would be a pretty shallow legacy."

It's ironic. When most people talked about legacy, money surfaced early in the conversation. However, as they probed deeper into the most meaningful parts of their legacies, money took a backseat. When describing what they hoped to give their loved ones, everyone, without exception, agreed with Steve (a father and grandfather) that money might be "the wrong game."

We may treat the money like it's the central part of our legacy, but when we focus on what we think really matters—books, articles, estate seminars, and professional urgings from attorneys, financial planners, and CPAs aside—it has nothing to do with money.

So, what is the "right game" according to the people I interviewed? Let's take a look.

What Matters to Us

I asked three generations this question: "What is your legacy to the people you love?" Here are the most recurring responses from the more than two hundred people who spoke with me:

I think the legacy my folks passed on to me and the one I would like to pass on to my kids is that midwestern ethic. You know—family, faith, and just a work ethic. Things you really don't think about.   —Jon, age 40

Instilling good morals. I've tried to teach my kids to be honest and have a sense of integrity.   —Judy, age 35

I hope my children can get from me what I didn't get from my parents. And that's how to live.   —Howard, age 69

Pride in being an American. My grandfather, who came here from the old country, used to listen to prizefights on the radio, and when the national anthem played, he would stand up in his living room and salute.   —John, age 57

I hope I taught them how to take care of themselves and to contribute to society.   —Helen, age 73

Relationships are what life is all about.   —Chris, age 45

That education is important.   —Gaile, age 81

A sense of peace. I would love for my family to know that.
I want them to have peace with their families and with
themselves.   —Shirley, age 60

The one thing I have tried to do is make them appreciate the
fact that they are alive and in good health. I have tried to
make them understand how fortunate they are.

—Elizabeth, age 72

My legacy? I want them to be hardworking kids. That's
important to me.

I don't know why. I guess it's because we were brought up
to be hard workers.   —Mary Lou, age 65

It all boils down to this: Parents hope they have helped to
make their children optimistic, happy, hardworking, and fam-
ily-centered men and women. As people got past the initial
difficulty of defining their legacy, they invariably said it had
everything to do with how their loved ones lived their lives
and nothing to do with how much money and how many
possessions they accumulated. When we talk about the people
we raise, encourage, and sacrifice for—those who give us so

much joy and cause us so much worry at the same time—we realize that, as Connie, a mother and grandmother, said, "It isn't a *legacy of the pocketbook* we want to give them, but rather a *legacy of the heart.*"

How do we know that we have successfully given our legacy of the heart? How do we know our loved ones understand that honesty, integrity, a family-first attitude, a work ethic, and other values are what really matter to us? We don't know. We rely on hope. We hope that we demonstrate to our loved ones what matters to us, and we hope they understand what they witness.

Hal, a retired grocer, said that instilling a sense of responsibility and self-sufficiency in his children was ". . . unspoken. I tried to show them by my example. I guess it's been a kind of unspoken legacy." Lorrie tried to "demonstrate my values to my two boys. I hope they got the message." Al said he has "tried to show Brian [his son] how I think he should live. But I'm not sure if he got it or not."

Above all else, we hope. And we hope in retrospect, not looking forward. No one had given their legacy more than a passing consideration until our interviews. But once people began to think and talk about it, their emotions flowed. Many people cried, some laughed nervously, and almost everyone struggled to articulate the legacy their parents had left them and the one they hope they have given their loved ones. Everyone who had raised children, from the first parent to the last, expressed regret that they didn't talk more often and openly with their loved ones about what they thought really mattered in life.

Demonstrating what is important certainly makes sense. But how can you be sure your children understand what you mean if you don't tell them? My father was on his ladder all those years, silently at work. Did he look down at me from the top of the ladder and hope that, by watching him, I would learn the importance of hard work? Is that what he wanted to give me? I don't know. His dedication to work often seemed like a wedge between the two of us, not like a legacy. He's been dead for years. I'll never know what he wanted for me. I live with the possibility that he didn't have anything at all in mind for me. I don't want to believe that. Unfortunately, the deafening silence during all those years indicates this could have been the case.

Clarify what matters to you. Then, practice bringing it down your ladder, rung by rung. When you finally say it out loud to the people you love, you instantly give them a part of your legacy that they will carry with them for the rest of their lives. No courts, lawyers, or readings of your will are required to pass on this part of your legacy to the people you love. You do it yourself. You do it every time you give them another story about the What of your life.

Howard's First Trip Down His Ladder

Let's bring a couple of "unspoken legacies," as Hal called them, down the ladder. We'll place them at the top of the ladder and practice bringing each one down, rung-by-rung.

Let's start with Howard, a retired postal worker and father of two daughters, each of whom has a family of her own. He said, "*I hope my children can get from me what I didn't get from my parents. And that's how to live.*" He went on to say that "how to live" means enjoying life, loving your family, and treating them with respect. But he hasn't told his daughters any of this. He's still high up on his ladder, keeping his thoughts to himself. Here's one way that Howard might begin, step-by-step, to transform his silent hopes into a conscious and powerful sharing of his thoughts with his daughters:

I hope my children can get from me what I didn't get from my parents. And that's how to live.

(Howard is at the top of the ladder, silently hoping his children "get" what is important to him.)

Lynn (and/or Mary), it's always been important to me and still is, that I help you to learn to live good and happy lives. . . .

(The first rung down: he starts by saying what's "important to me." This sets the tone for a sharing of the What of his life.)

Because I didn't get that from my parents and I know now it caused me a lot of heartache in life. . . .

(Then he tells them why it's important to him.)

My parents didn't talk to me. They didn't tell me what they thought was important in life or what they wanted for me. They never said and I never asked. . . .

(He is willing to give his daughters a glimpse into a difficult part of his child-hood he probably would prefer not to talk about.)

Continued

After all these years, I realize I haven't been very good at talking with you either. I haven't told you what I thought was important in life or what I wanted for you. . . .

It's taken me a long time to realize what was most important in my own life. I wish I could turn back the clock to when you were little girls and tell you this, but the best I can do is to tell you now. . . .

(As he moves farther down the ladder, his remarks become more intimate and personal.)

I want you to be happy and content in your lives in a way I never was until now. I want you to experience that joy sooner than I did. I haven't told you before, but. . . .

I am so proud of how loving and open you are with your children. You show your love without being embarrassed or ashamed. You talk with them in a way I never did with you or even dreamed was possible. . . .

(It's a conversation filled with "I." What *you* think and feel is the foundation of your legacy of the heart.)

I think that may be the most important gift you give your children. . . .

And it's something I still want to give you. After all these years, I am finally able to start telling you how much you mean to me and that I am the happiest and most content when I am with you.

(Howard is not simply reminiscing about what should have been. He defines his legacy going forward from here.)

Howard's first trip down the ladder probably won't be an easy one. He may fumble a little as he searches for a way to express his thoughts out loud. He may be nervous, which could cause him to rush down the ladder faster than he should. But think how good he will feel to be off that ladder for the first time.

The next time down will be easier for him. And the time after that will be even easier. He will learn how to let his loved ones ask questions and even show their uneasiness with or disapproval of what he has to say. It will take practice. But before long, he'll step down that ladder with confidence and ease. He'll become adept at knowing when to talk and when to listen.

This first trip down the ladder to bring his loved ones a taste of what's important in his life will be followed by many more. Maybe the next time he will continue to expand on some part of what he said during his first trip down the ladder. For example, maybe he'll say, "I want to tell you why I didn't talk to you more when you were children. I was just too consumed with work and. . . . " Or maybe his next trip down will involve an entirely different part of his life, like which person mattered to him the most when he was a child. Or maybe what event in his life had the biggest impact on him. He'll find plenty to share with his daughters.

After all, he has lived a long life, and up to now he's kept most of it a secret.

He's got a lot of talking to do to let his two girls learn who he is and what he thinks their life together really means.

Mary Lou's First Trip Down Her Ladder

Mary Lou, a mother of three adult boys said, "My legacy? I want them to be hardworking kids. That's important to me. I don't know why. I guess it's because we were brought up to be hard workers."

Mary Lou has never told her children that hard work is important to her. She assumed they learned by watching her and their dad, Ron, who died a few years ago. Now she wants to tell them. First, she needs to spend a few minutes clarifying in her own mind why hard work matters to her. Let's assume she has done so and is ready to tell her boys. She decides to begin with Ralph, her oldest son:

I want them to be hardworking kids. That's important to me. I don't know why. I guess it's because we were brought up to be hard workers.

(Mary Lou is near the top of her ladder, trying to articulate why having hard-working kids is important to her.)

Ralph, it's important to me that you know how much I value hard work. I assumed all these years that by watching your dad and me, you already knew. But lately, I've realized I wasn't even sure. I've thought about it and I'm able to tell you why hard work has been so important to me. . . .

(She takes her first step down. She talks face-to-face with Ralph. She admits she had to figure out why hard work is so important to her. She's done that and now she wants to be sure he also knows.)

I feel that hard work reflects effort. And effort reflects your attitude about life. I think that hardworking people show their willingness to be engaged in life. . . .

(She begins to tell her son what makes hard work so important to her.)

Rich or poor, I think people need to work hard. One of the reasons I worked so hard was to give you some advantages I never had. . . .

(She continues to flesh out the meaning that hard work has for her.)

But another reason, just as important to me, was to teach you by my example that willingness to work is a measure of a person's character. . . .

I hope I accomplished that. You have always been a hard worker and I am proud of you for that. I hope you pass on the value of hard work to your children. . . .

Continued

But I also hope that you will tell them. Don't assume that just by watching, they will understand what matters to you. Tell them, so you can be sure they have every opportunity to really understand, or they can ask you questions if they don't. . . .

(She encourages him to say out loud to his children what matters to him.)

I would like to tell you, your brothers, and the grandkids other things that are important in my life. I've started to take an inventory of sorts of what really matters to me. I'd like to start sharing this with all of you.

(Going forward, Mary Lou intends to share her legacy with her grandchildren too.)

What piece of her legacy will Mary Lou take down the ladder next time? Maybe she'll continue to talk about the importance she places on work. Or maybe she will tell her grandchildren about the math teacher in high school who took a special interest in her and helped transform her from a below-average student to an honors graduate who was awarded an academic scholarship to college. Maybe she'll tell them about one of her proudest moments: the day she took her elderly mother home from the hospital and cared for her until her death several months later.

It's possible that her openness will encourage her children and grandchildren to ask her to bring something down the ladder that they had wondered about but never before mentioned. Maybe her granddaughter Jenny will even feel comfortable enough to ask a question that's been on her mind for months: why her grandmother gives so much money to charity when she doesn't have enough to buy a new car. What to say and how to say it will get easier for Mary Lou after a few trips down the ladder. Each trip down will also make it easier for her loved ones to listen and to react openly and honestly to what she has to say.

The First Trip Down Your Ladder

Now it's your turn. Go back to your top three "What" questions that you identified from the list on pages 34–35. Choose one of the three and try bringing it down the ladder. Before you begin, here are some dos and don'ts that might make coming down the ladder easier and more enjoyable for you.

Do:

- Adopt the same format we used earlier with Howard and Mary Lou. Dissect what is important to you, rung-by-rung. Before long, you probably won't need to put your thoughts in writing; you'll be comfortable doing it in your head.
- Practice saying it out loud, as if you were talking to your loved ones.
- Of the three questions you chose, start with the one that seems the "safest" to talk about. By safe, I mean something that is not emotionally charged for you or your loved ones. Launching into a discussion of all the suppressed resentment you have about your daughter's alcoholic ex-husband is likely to provoke a higher level of

anxiety than a story about how proud you are that she has raised two wonderful children by herself. In the beginning, it will be easier to bring something small down the ladder. Save the tough topics for later, when you have more experience talking and they have more experience listening.

Don't:

- Overthink the exercise. Choose one of the three questions and begin taking it down the ladder.
- Worry that you can't fill all the rungs of the ladder. Your ladder may have five rungs the first time and fifteen the next. Practice your descent without judging your performance.
- Agonize over the significance of what you have chosen. If it matters to you, don't worry that your loved ones might think it's unimportant.

Use the ladder on the next two pages or draw your own. On the top rung of the ladder, write what is important to you. Then, take the first step down by restating the same thought on the next rung as if you were talking to a loved one, just like Howard and Mary Lou did. Use as many rungs as you need to flesh out your thoughts. Add more rungs if you need them. Remember, this is a practice run in preparation for the first time you say it face-to-face to a loved one. Good luck!

(Name), *I want to tell you what I think about* _____

_____

_____

_____

This matters to me because _____

_____

_____

_____

_____

_____

_____

_____

Continued

5

Knowing Why You Live
the Way You Do

Have you ever written an autobiographical sketch of yourself? Try it. At the very least, it helps you reach back to many forgotten events and decisions in your life. Here's my autobiography, a bare-bones retrospective sketch that I jotted down in less than fifteen minutes:

I was born in Kingston, a small town in upstate New York. I grew up in a blue-collar family, the second youngest of four sisters and a brother. We lived in the same house for twenty years. My father was a lineman for the telephone company for forty-two years and my mother was a homemaker. I received a B.A. in English from Siena College in Albany, New York, and a doctorate in education from Syracuse University. After completing my doctoral degree, I was the director of a community living program for handicapped people in Louisville, Kentucky. I then moved to Colorado Springs, Colorado, where I taught elementary school and spent several years as a public-school administrator. At the age of thirty-nine, I changed careers, became a certified financial planner, and worked at a national brokerage firm and in my own business. After thirteen years in financial planning, I decided to return to education and became Director of Education at a psychiatric facility.

I have written several books and articles on subjects ranging from investing overseas to family relationships. I have volunteered at a local nursing home and a domestic violence program. My wife, Amy, and I have four sons, Eamon, Seth, Conor, and Thomas. My favorite activities are writing, golfing, Sunday morning donuts with my sons, going to movies with my wife, watching the History Channel, and taking Saturday afternoon naps on the couch.

As I reread it one day, I realized my autobiographical sketch was a gold mine of unsaid Whys. I was stunned at all the Whys of my life that I had neglected to share with my loved ones. Why I was proud of my blue-collar background.

Why I earned a doctorate in education. Why I became a teacher and an administrator in public schools. Why I worked with handicapped people as a young man. Why I switched careers to become a financial planner. Why I recently returned to education. Why I spend so much time painstakingly writing and rewriting drafts of chapters for books and magazine articles. Why I give some of my time to help people in need.

And how about the Why of the family I love so much? I hadn't divulged much of that either. Why my wife and I married. Why we decided to have children. Why we live in Colorado. Why we chose the neighborhood and house we live in.

It's not just the big events in my life that I haven't discussed with my loved ones. It's the seemingly less important activities of my life, too. Why I rarely watch anything on television other than the History Channel, much to the amusement of my four boys. Why I treasure those Saturday afternoon naps. Why I like our "boys out" Sunday morning ritual of donuts and milk at the nearby Dunkin' Donuts shop. Why I like golf outings with them and movies with their mom. Big stuff and little stuff, it all defines me. My kids were watching me live my life and were even participating in a large part of it. But rarely, if ever, did I tell them why I behaved like I did. Maybe they knew why; maybe they didn't. I was sure of one thing. Up to that point in our lives together, if I unexpectedly went to my grave, my epitaph could have been:

He lived and died and never said "why."

That was not how I wanted my loved ones to remember me. I decided to start talking to my kids about myself. If that's an epitaph you might be stuck with, you too can change it by starting to talk.

First, try sketching your autobiography. Make it brief and make it about *you*. This is an exercise in "I." Think of it as a quick inventory of some of the places and events of your life that immediately come to mind. Don't worry about omitting something important. Make it easy and fun—a fifteen- to thirty-minute stroll down memory lane. This is not about correct grammar, sentence structure, neatness, or anything else your high-school English teacher taught you. Simply try, as effortlessly as you can, to recall some of the Whys of your life, both big and little. Use the back of an envelope or the other side of an old shopping list, if you wish. Just start jotting down your thoughts.

After you are done, ask yourself how diligent you have
been in giving the Why of your life to the people you love.
Does your self-inventory include lots of unsaid Whys? In
Chapter 4, you learned how to begin the transfer of your
"legacy of the heart" by bringing what matters in your life
down the ladder. Now, you'll learn how to complete the giving
of yourself by bringing the Why of your life—why you live
life the way you do—down the same ladder.

They Really Do Wonder Why

Rose still wonders why her father, who died twenty years ago,
didn't pursue a career in the field he loved the most:

> I know my father went to a radio school in Chicago during
> the 1930s. He loved radios. They were his true passion. But he
> and my mother came back to Canon City to live. That's where
> my dad was originally from. He worked as a prison guard. I'm
> not sure why. Maybe that's the only work he could find.

Greg, now thirty-eight years old, wonders why his favorite
grandmother went into a nursing home:

I remember my grandmother wanting to move in with us, but my dad wouldn't let her. She was a fantastic person. My mother told me that Dad didn't want her living with us. That really bothered me. I never found out why she wasn't allowed to live with us.

Ron still wonders why his eighty-five-year-old parents keep themselves isolated from other people:

My parents have always been loners. Even as a kid, I wondered why they didn't want to socialize. People would invite them to their homes, but they would never go. I still wonder why they seem so negative about other people.

Sharon wishes her retired parents would spend some money on themselves. She wonders why they don't:

I hope they are not saving it for me. I don't need it. I want them to enjoy it. But they don't spend a dime on themselves. I know my mom would love to travel a little. They have more than they will ever need.

Susan has never stopped wondering about the blessing her father gave before each family meal:

It sounds silly, but I never understood why my father gave this quick blessing: "Lord, we thank thee for this food and for all you have given us." He was not a particularly religious person. Neither was my mother. But every night Dad said that same blessing. I remember it made me kind of uncomfortable. It seemed out of place.

And Bob, a forty-eight-year-old father of four children, carried this worry with him throughout his childhood because his father didn't tell him why:

My mother was Catholic and raised us all in the Church. She went to Mass almost every day. My dad never went to church. Every Sunday, he would drive us all to church and sit in the car and read the newspaper. We'd come out, and he took us back home. This went on Sunday after Sunday for years. And you know what? . . . I had no idea why.

I knew nothing about my dad's religious background or beliefs. He never told me what he thought about God or why he wouldn't go to church with us. One day in second grade, I screwed up enough courage to ask the nun—I went to a Catholic grade school—what would happen to my father if he wasn't a Catholic, or worse yet, if he didn't even believe in God. She looked at me, shook her head and said, "All we can do is pray for him." I'll never forget it. To me, that meant my dad was going straight to hell when he died. I carried that worry with me for years. I used to think, "My dad doesn't go to church. He might not even believe in God. I have to pray for him so he doesn't go to hell. But what if my prayers don't work? Then sure enough, he will end up in hell!" It used to worry me to death. I didn't know what to do about it.

These are some of the Whys children are left wondering and fretting about, often for the rest of their lives. Whys about work, relationships, spirituality, money, and even family rituals can leave huge gaps in a child's understanding of a parent's life and their lives together. Rose, Greg, Ron, Sharon, Susan, and Bob could describe what they saw, and in some cases how uncomfortable or worrisome it was for them, but not why it happened. Their parents left the Why of these events unsaid. How much of the Why of your life remains unspoken?

The Nature of a "Why"

Just like saying what is important to you requires practice, so too does revealing why you live the way you do. And like the What of your life, the Why might not always be easy for you to recognize or articulate. Until I asked myself why, I was never sure why I'm drawn to world history. Or why I left education, my field of training, to become a thirty-nine-year-old rookie in the investment business.

My wife Amy has devoted seventeen years of her life to public education, first as a teacher and now as an elementary-school principal. She is passionate about the well-being of her staff and students. But when I asked her why she chose teaching as her profession and why she chose to become a principal, with its long hours and constant pressure to produce high test scores, she said, "I think I became a teacher because I like working with children. . . . I'm not sure. And why am I a principal? I don't really know. You get so immersed in the doing of it every day, you don't stop to think about why you're there in the first place."

We do many things in the course of our lives, some significant and some not, without knowing for certain why we do them. Some have been part of our everyday behavior for years and yet we still don't know why we do them. As Amy said, "you get so immersed in the doing of it" that the underlying "Why" never gets the thought it deserves.

Let's dissect the nature of a Why. Doing so can make telling it to others a much easier task. When you examine why you live life the way you do, keep in mind that:

- Examining the Why means looking at your behavior. Why you do the things you do, both big and little. Why you go to work every day. Why you chose your current profession. Why you don't go to the doctor when you are sick. Why you read the sports section first. Why you abhor crowded restaurants but eagerly look forward to sitting in a football stadium packed with 50,000 people.

- You probably won't know the Whys your loved ones wonder about unless you start talking first. They probably won't ask. Identify the Whys of your life and begin bringing them down the ladder. When you do, your loved ones will be more comfortable coming forward with the Whys they want to know about.

- Sometimes the Whys you consider the most insignificant are the ones your loved ones wonder about the most. Don't take for granted that they are not interested in a Why just because it seems trivial to you.

- Some Whys are easier to talk about than others. Start with the easy Whys. Learn how to bring them down the ladder before you tackle the harder ones.

- Not all of the Whys of your life were good decisions. You are a master of articulating "Why" when you can talk with ease and comfort about the Whys that you regret or that might not flatter you.

- If you don't know Why, say so. Your loved ones get to know you better when you admit that sometimes you also wonder why.

Bringing a "Little" Why Down the Ladder

Let's dissect a small Why. My kids, especially my oldest boy, give me a good-natured dose of kidding about my interest in the History Channel. I thought that behind the jokes, my son Eamon might really wonder why I am such a devotee of the past. So I decided to bring my passion for history down the ladder and share it with Eamon. Here's how I did it:

Gee, Dad, not another World War II show. Dad, you don't need to keep watching. I can tell you how it turns out. We won!

(Eamon kids me about my interest in history. It will probably always be a source of good-natured kidding between us.)

Continued

Eamon, I never told you why I like all this history stuff. . . .

(But here's an opportunity to say why I do "keep watching." I start taking this Why down the ladder.)

I realize that I've always been drawn to it—even when I was your age. My favorite subject in high school was American history, especially the world wars we were involved in. . . .

(I tell my son that it's an interest I had at his age. I had never before told him that.)

You see me watching World War II footage on the History Channel, and you know, I wasn't even alive during the war. But your mom's dad fought in that war. If you watch these films, you can see what he went through. . . .

(Eamon learns a little more about his grandfather. This is not a subject his grandpa mentions.)

And the elderly men you see now in their seventies and eighties, you might never know what many of them went through if you didn't watch the films, because they don't talk much about it. . . .

Many were only eighteen- or nineteen-year-old boys who had never been away from home. The next thing they knew, they were overseas fighting a world war. . . .

I watch the films partly out of interest but also because of respect and admiration for what those guys did—men like your grandpa. . . .

(As I come farther down the ladder, Eamon learns that this is not just mindless TV watching for me. I'm not sure he knew—or that I did either!)

Continued

Sometimes, I wonder if I could do what they did. I think I could, but I'm not sure. . . .

(It even makes me take stock of myself—"Could I do it?" I'm comfortable telling him that I'm not sure I could.)

Eamon, it's only recently that I really thought about this. You and I joking about my interest in history has caused me to ask myself why I am drawn to it.

(Eamon learns that he has played a part in prodding me to uncover the Why of this small piece of my life. He knows more about how I think and feel. Coming down the ladder, even with something this trivial, brings us a little closer together.)

It was an easy, relaxed unveiling of a Why of my life. I enjoyed bringing my TV habits down the ladder to Eamon. We still joke about my fascination with the past. But we have put some meat on the bones of this small piece of my life. My son knows more about what makes me tick. Big or small, part of my legacy to Eamon is making sure I have given him an understanding of why I live my life the way I do.

Bringing a "Big" Why Down the Ladder

Now let's bring a big Why down the ladder. Let's deal with something emotionally charged and, consequently, probably more difficult to discuss. Earlier in this chapter, Bob spoke about his mother's devotion to the Catholic Church. She raised all the children to be devout Catholics. On the other hand, his dad, now deceased, neither attended church nor talked about his spiritual beliefs. Each Sunday, Bob's mom attended Mass with all five children while their father waited in the car. Not once did either parent tell Bob why his dad read the paper while they were in church.

Bob still hypothesizes about the Why of that Sunday morning ritual. Based on his sense of who his dad was and a discussion with his elderly aunt (his dad's sister), Bob explained his theory about why his father never once walked through the doors of Saint Mary's Church with the rest of the family. I'll share Bob's thinking with you. But I'll do it as if his dad were talking to Bob when he was a boy. The ladder below shows how Bob's father might have explained why he was not a participant in the spiritual life of his family:

Sunday morning, back home from church. However, today is different. Bob's dad suggests they have a game of catch in the backyard. As they toss the ball back and forth, Bob's dad begins to come down his ladder.

Bob, every Sunday you're in church and I'm waiting for you in the car. I don't think I've ever told you why I don't go to church. *Now I want to tell you why. . . .*

(Bob's dad calmly starts to bring this emotional matter down the ladder.)

When I was a kid, my parents
were pretty rigid about a lot of
things. We had to get dressed up
for dinner. I had to wear a jacket
and tie every night. Dad was a
stern guy. I think that's how he
was raised by his parents. . . .

(You don't always paint a
rosy picture when you
reveal the Why.)

Church was harsh too. I didn't
like it. The pastor was a fire-and-
brimstone preacher—always talking about how we were going to
end up in hell. . . .

I rebelled. When I was a teenager, I refused to go to church
anymore. I'd had enough. I think
it was a way for me to get back
at my parents too. . . .

(It's OK for a parent to say
he/she was not a perfect
child or teenager.)

Continued

97

And I've never been back to church. But I want you to know that I do believe in God. I pray to him. But I don't go to church to do it. . . .

(He lets Bob know for the first time that he does believe in God.)

Your mom and I agreed that all you kids would be brought up in the Catholic Church. That's a big part of your mom's faith and I respect and support that. . . .

(And he reveals that he and Bob's mom have discussed this—something Bob never knew before.)

But for me, my praying is done in private. . . .

You know Bob, I'm not just reading the paper in the car while you are in church. I'm saying my prayers too.

(By taking just a few steps down the ladder, he has given Bob an initial understanding of a very important and personal part of his life.)

Imagine how much Bob learned about his dad during a quick game of catch in the backyard. Bob discovered why his dad doesn't go to church, that he believes in God, that he has talked about this with Bob's mom, and that he even says his own prayers. Now, when Bob is in church, he can picture his dad praying in the car.

Imagine the sense of relief Bob might have felt from this three-minute conversation with his father. Maybe his dad was OK in God's eyes after all. Maybe he wasn't going to hell, and maybe Bob didn't have to say enough of the right prayers to get his father to heaven.

And think about all the avenues of future discussion this short trip down the ladder could have generated between father and son. It might have laid the groundwork for discussions about his dad's life as a child, why his grandfather was so stern, why his dad rebelled against his parents and how they reacted, and on and on. Who knows? Unveiling just this one Why might have triggered the beginning of a much deeper relationship between Bob and his father.

It's Your Turn Again

Refer back to your top three Why questions from the list on pages 37–38. Choose the question that seems to be the safest to discuss—the one that seems the least emotionally charged for both you and your loved ones and the easiest for you to articulate. Try bringing it down the ladder on the next two pages. Take the same approach you used in the last chapter to bring a What down the ladder. On the first rung, write the Why you are about to discuss. On the second rung, begin to take it down the ladder. Use as few or as many rungs as you wish. Remember, you are not actually talking to anyone yet; this is just a dry run down the ladder. Be totally open and honest. Write what you are really thinking:

(Name), *I want you to know why I* _____

_____

_____

_____

I do (don't do) it because _____

_____

_____

_____

6

Saying the What and Why Out Loud

Sometimes, Just a Few Words Can Move Mountains

After my mother died, my father had a lot of time on his hands, so he wrote his autobiography. It was very well done. He liked to write. Actually, his job was writing owners' manuals for Maytag appliances. He seemed to like it. But he had a history of heart problems and, toward the end, he was in pretty bad health. I think he might have written his autobiography because he wanted us to learn what he went through during his life. I don't know. But he left us his story. I really need to sit down and read it more thoroughly than I have in the past.

Art is a fifty-five-year-old maintenance supervisor for a public-school system. He grew up in Long Island, New York. He remembers his dad as "interested in the well-being of his family. A very hard worker, a religious man, not a real emotional guy, not very open. He kept everything in." Art recalled his surprise when he received a copy of his father's autobiography in the mail. After more than fifty years, he never expected his dad to share the particulars of his life. But here it was, the written story of his father's life. Art had never heard most of it before.

For example, Art discovered that his dad "at one point in his life, was ashamed of his name. My father wrote that when he was a young man, people discriminated against him because of his Italian heritage." Art found out that it caused a "crisis period in his life." His dad's written story of himself gave Art a rare opportunity to peek behind the curtains a little into the life of the man who raised him.

Although Art was surprised to receive his dad's autobiography, it didn't seem to have much importance to him. In fact, two years after his dad sent it to him, Art still hadn't given it a thorough reading. He talked about it as if his dad had finally cleaned out the attic of their old house, piled a bunch of dusty relics from the past into a box and said, "Here Art, this is yours." I could picture Art looking through the box, politely thanking his dad, while at the same time thinking: "Why did he give me this box of old stuff? Did he really think it was important for me to have it? Or did he just want to get rid of it? Did he do it for my benefit, or his own?"

Why did Art's dad write his story? Art wondered about this the day it arrived in the mail. Two years later he still wonders why. Art hopes his dad wrote it because he felt it was important for his family to learn more about his life. But he might have written it simply because he "had a lot of time on his hands" and "liked to write." Think of the impact the autobiography might have had on Art's life if his dad had said something like: "Art, this is for you. I want you to know more about who I am. I want you to learn about some of the important events in my life that I don't think you know much about. I have always liked to write. Now I have written something for you. I have written the story of my life for you." Then, Art might have treated it like a precious gift instead of a box of assorted odds and ends that had been dragged out of the attic.

If his father had said out loud in just a sentence or two why he wrote his autobiography, it might have been his greatest gift to his son and one of Art's most treasured possessions.

Is it far-fetched to think that a few words spoken from the heart of an old man could plant the seeds for a new relationship with a middle-aged son? That's exactly what happened to Jerry, who told me this wonderful story:

My father and I were never close. He was a tough old Norwegian farmer from Minnesota. It just wasn't in his genes to show his feelings. He wasn't mean to me or physical with me when I was a kid, or anything like that. He just didn't seem to like being with me. I can remember going bird hunting with him. It just wasn't much fun. He wouldn't talk to me. He always seemed to be brooding. All of these years I thought it was me. What else would I think? So, I got out of there as soon as I was eighteen. I went off to college. And our relationship remained distant and strained for the next forty years.

He flew out to visit us [Jerry and his family] about four years ago. It was right after my mother had died, so he was living alone. I had just read something about trying to resolve conflicts with your elderly parents before they die. I decided to thank him for doing such a good job providing for us kids when he and Mom had so little money. So I did. And you wouldn't believe how this caused him to open up. I only talked with him about five or six minutes, but he just opened up. I was amazed at what he was worrying about all these years. When I was sixteen, I told my father I was done with the Lutheran Church. I just wasn't going anymore. He said, "Oh, okay." He never said anything more about it. Then we had this talk—now I'm fifty-six and he's in his early eighties [laughs]—you know what he said to me? "We wondered about you and the Church. We have been worried about you ever since you stopped attending." I told him not to worry, that I took the good from the Church and applied it to my life. He said, "Oh, good. That's what we thought." And you could see this sense of relief on his face. He had been carrying this around for more than forty years. By me telling him he did pretty good as a provider for his family, it freed him up to tell me what was on his mind. And you know, it gave me a whole different look at him.

That was the beginning of us finally talking with each other. My dad died a few months ago. But the last four years were the best years we had together. We only saw each other a couple of times a year and we'd talk on the phone now and then, but we could talk about ourselves and each other. He didn't dislike me after all. We found a respect for each other and developed a closeness that made those last few years with him something I won't ever forget.

Forty years of silence and misunderstanding began melting away after less than ten minutes of open exchange between an elderly father and his middle-aged son. For the first time, Jerry found out his dad actually worried about him. For the first time, his dad found out Jerry thought he did a good job as a father. A fairly simple exchange of words between the two led to a remarkable outcome. Jerry and his dad created a new kind of relationship that they enjoyed for four years. A relationship built on a few long-overdue words of honesty changed how they viewed each other and their relationship together.

It might have turned out the same way for Art, if his father had been able to deliver his autobiography along with a few words of intimacy and honesty. And so too it can turn out that way for you and a loved one, regardless of how many years of silence and separation have passed, if the message is finally delivered. It doesn't have to be lengthy, profound, or eloquent. As Jerry found out, sometimes it just has to be said.

Trust Your Thoughts

My son Conor is a scratch golfer. This means that on average he takes only seventy-two shots to complete a par seventy-two course. So, he is a very talented player. I, on the other hand, am not. I rarely break a hundred. I'm one of those weekend hackers with a beautiful practice swing. Then the moment of truth arrives. I have to hit the ball. As I stand over that little white ball, I think too much about hitting it exactly the right way; my body tightens, and my swing deteriorates. I have taken dozens of lessons and committed to memory all the mechanics of a good golf swing. But knowing how to properly swing the club has not made me a good player. Unfortunately, I still have to hit the ball!

Conor and I were at the practice range on a Saturday afternoon, and as I stood there exasperated and desperate, I asked him what one piece of advice he would give to help me become a better player. He said, "Dad, I think part of your problem is you've gotten too much advice. You're trying to remember too many things at once, and you get so tense, you can hardly start the club back. You have a nice swing. Trust it. You are so worried about hitting a bad shot, you can't hit a good one. You know how to swing the club, but when you stand over the ball, you think too much about what can go wrong. You have to step up to the ball and hit it. Just trust your swing."

Conor's words hit home. He was right. I do know how to hit a golf ball. But I am so worried about hitting a bad shot, I rarely hit a good one. I need to think less, walk up to the ball, and hit it. Just as Conor suggested, I need to trust my swing.

In the last two chapters, you practiced how to bring the What and Why of your life down the ladder. Now, you need to tell your stories to the people you love. You can spend so much time thinking about just the right way to say the What and Why that you never say them. Or you get so nervous and uptight, you can't say them with the openness and ease that makes the experience enjoyable and meaningful for you and your loved ones. Don't spend too much time on the practice range analyzing your thoughts. Step up and say what feels right. Trust your thoughts.

Down the Ladder You Come . . .
and Away They Run

Well, I did what I told you I was going to do. While we were
on vacation, I asked each of my three boys what they thought
about me. I don't know if I scared them or not [laughs]. The
oldest boy changed the subject right away. The middle boy
shot back with: "Gosh, Mom, what kind of a question is
that?" and walked away. And the youngest boy said, "I don't
know right off the top of my head. Let me think about it."

During our first interview, it occurred to Marlene that she
had never asked her three adult sons what they thought about
her. She was determined to find out. When they were together
at a family reunion a few weeks later, she asked each of them.
Marlene saw it as a fairly simple and straightforward question.
But none of the boys gave a direct answer. Her oldest son
evaded the question, the middle son seemed annoyed, and the
youngest one tried to put her off. As you might expect,
Marlene was disappointed and even a little discouraged that
none of her boys had an answer for her.

Think about living in a parent-child relationship that's forty years old. A relationship in which people never asked questions like: "What do you think about me?" A relationship in which you were much more likely to discuss what was for dinner than how you felt about each other. Suddenly, with no warning, your mother or father says, "I want to know what you think about me." Yikes! Maybe that's why none of Marlene's sons could respond on the spot to such a personal and intimate question. Maybe it was so unexpected and so far outside the boundaries of typical interactions with their mother that one instinctively ducked, one growled, and one stalled for time!

I cannot imagine my dad bolting down his ladder one hot summer afternoon and saying, "Bill, I'm going to stop burning and scraping and painting the house for a few minutes. I want to ask you something. I'd like to know how you feel about me." I think I would have slowly backed away from the ladder, turned, and run for cover behind the back bushes. It would have been too much of an emotional leap for me to make. Years of mostly small talk, functional conversation, and an occasional admonishment or warning, suddenly replaced with such an intimate and personal question! I simply couldn't have responded. I barely could have tolerated hearing the question.

Don't set yourself up for failure by rushing down your ladder at your loved ones.

Here are some ways to smooth the path so you and your loved ones can engage in a pattern of communication that will increase the likelihood that when you talk, they will be able to listen.

- Most important of all, remember to begin the conversation by talking about you, not asking them to answer questions. Marlene tried to start a conversation with her sons by asking each of them to answer her question, "What do you think about me?" As she suggested when recalling the disappointing results, she probably unnerved them with such a pointed question. Not only did her question put each boy on the spot, it required a response that would have made each of them vulnerable in the presence of his mother.

  Marlene might have had more success if she began the conversation by showing that she was willing to talk about herself instead of expecting answers from them. Then, her sons would have seen that she was willing take the risk and make herself vulnerable in their presence instead of expecting them to be the first to do so. For many parents, this is a role reversal that's difficult to put into practice. When we talk with our children, we are used to probing, directing, and instructing, not talking about ourselves.

Remember this cardinal rule of how to initiate a conversation about the What and Why of you life: Talk about yourself, don't ask them to do the talking.

- Break the ice with a positive and safe conversation. You'll each stay more relaxed and able to communicate if you talk about a What or Why that is nonthreatening to both of you. "I think I've been so blessed to have you as a son" would have been a much safer and upbeat lead-in for Marlene to begin a conversation with each of her sons than, "What do you think of me?" From that more comfortable starting point, she could begin disclosing the impact that each of them has had on her life. And from there, all of them would be in a better frame of mind to tackle increasingly sensitive subjects and questions. Positive, complimentary conversations make people feel safe and consequently better able to listen when you talk.

- Keep it short, especially in the beginning. You both might need to build a tolerance for having a "real" conversation with each other. So, don't overpower your loved ones with an hour-long sit-down discussion about your life. You will probably do most of the sharing of the What and Why of your life in bits and pieces during the natural course of everyday interactions with your loved ones. A minute or

two here or there will probably be enough to give the gift
of you to the people you love.

- Talk when the time seems right. Be careful with this.
  Choose what seems like a good time to talk, but don't
  insist on waiting for *the* perfect one. For example, it might
  be better to talk with your daughter on the phone while
  your twin grandsons are at school, rather than at nine
  o'clock at night, when they are in the background complaining that it's too early to go to bed. If possible, talk
  when you are both relaxed and thus can better listen to
  each other. But with that said, don't keep putting it off
  until just the right time. We are all so busy, there is never a
  perfect time. Just be aware of the best opportunities during
  the day for your conversation and seize the moment.

- Treat the sharing of the What and Why of your life as a
  process, not a catharsis. Like Marlene, you can become so
  excited at the prospect of having a real conversation with
  your loved ones that you rush at them with your thoughts
  and feelings and they instinctively run the other way.
  Don't be discouraged if your newfound excitement to talk
  is not met with an equally enthusiastic willingness to listen. Be patient. Take your time. Treat the sharing of your
  life like a marathon, not a sprint. Remember, you and

your loved ones might be accustomed to standing at opposite ends of the ladder. You might find that you and your son or daughter engage in a meaningful conversation one day followed by an eminently forgettable one the next. Keep at it. It takes time to redefine old boundaries. Expect plenty of ups and downs along the way.

- No matter how many steps you take to pave the way for a comfortable and productive conversation, anticipate a range of unpredictable reactions from your loved ones. One may embrace what you have to say. Another might seem uninterested, uncomfortable, unwilling to listen, or even visibly upset. In fact, regardless of how skillfully and diplomatically you present what you have to say, some of your loved ones might never listen.

To paraphrase the old saying about a horse and water, "You can lead a loved one to the gift of you, but you can't make him (or her) accept it." Enjoy your successes with those that embrace your gift, but also take satisfaction in knowing that you tried with those who can't or won't listen.

They Can't Learn How to Listen If You Don't Talk

We have had some heart-to-heart talks, but not very often. Kids' attention spans are not real long, especially as they get into their

middle teenage years. They consider it more of a lecture than
anything else.   —Charlie, father of a sixteen-year-old

There are a lot of stories I won't be able to share with my kids
until they are older. Just like other kids the same age, their
attention spans are limited.

—Josh, father of an eight-year-old and a six-year-old

Beware of self-fulfilling prophecies. If you assume they don't
want to or can't listen, then they probably won't. If you expect
disinterest, you are likely to get it. They can listen when they
think they should. If they can pay attention for forty-five minutes in math class at school, they can listen to you tell a three-
minute story about yourself. They can and they will, especially if
it relates to their own interests and concerns. For example, your
eleven-year-old might want to know what you were like in elementary school. Did you worry, like he does, about being the
last kid picked by your classmates for the dodgeball game? Were
you ever picked last? How did you handle it?

What if your teenager, who suddenly seems unwilling to
share anything with you other than name, rank, and serial
number, silently wonders what high school was like for you.
Were you popular in school? Did you date much? How did you
afford to buy all the clothes you needed in order to "look

right"? Weren't some of the subjects you took in high school really a waste of your time too? You can have a lot of fun with these kinds of stories. When you tell stories that they relate to, you'll loosen up and so will they.

Once again, remember that all-important rule of effective communication before you begin talking—you are about to tell your loved ones how you live *your* life, not how they should live theirs. Guard against the parental urge to shift your story from a discussion of your life to a set of recommendations about theirs. Betty, a sixty-three-year-old mother of two grown children, said it best: "When you are raising your kids, you are giving lectures all the time. You don't intend to, but you are. You are constantly . . . I don't know . . . telling them things."

Telling a story about yourself is markedly different from delivering a lecture about how they should act. Lectures foster short attention spans. But if you can share the What and Why of your life, especially if you can do so with warts and all, they will sense your honesty and openness and have a much easier time listening.

If you turn the What and Why of your life into a morality play, they'll probably tune you out. George Washington chopped down the cherry tree and supposedly said, "I cannot tell a lie." True or not, as a child I remember having difficulty relating to what seemed like an unrealistic and contrived dose of morality. I wondered if, after chopping down the cherry tree, George didn't at least try to pin it on his brother before he finally confessed. As a child, this certainly would have seemed like a more believable story to me.

Tell real stories about yourself. Don't sanitize them beyond the point of recognition. Let your loved ones see who you *really* are. What you think about. What truly matters to you. How you made some of the same mistakes they make. How you dealt with some of the same worries and embarrassments they deal with.

My sixteen-year-old stepson Seth recently experienced his first rejection by a girl. He met Jessica at the ice cream store where they both worked. I never saw a teenager so eager to get to work each day! But the romance was short-lived. Jessica abruptly dumped Seth, and he felt hurt, angry, and terribly embarrassed. He struggled with the reality of having to return to work and face Jessica and his coworkers. My reaction was to give Seth the plenty-of-other-fish-in-the-sea speech. You know, the standard response that he'll meet lots of other girls and find somebody much nicer than the one who just jilted him. Looking back, I realize that my canned "don't worry about it" response to Seth's distress was due to my own discomfort. He was upset and I didn't know how to handle it. So I ducked behind a benign but meaningless response to Seth's dilemma.

Thankfully, my wife, Amy, had a more thoughtful and personal reaction. She told him a story about a boy she dated in college. Here's what she said to Seth: Her boyfriend began flirting with another girl at a college dance. He left Amy standing alone on the dance floor and went home with the other girl. Amy told Seth she avoided everyone for days afterward because she was so humiliated. She was sure she was the laughingstock of her dormitory. And to make matters worse, for months afterward she saw her ex-boyfriend every day in class. Amy told Seth that her sense of anguish slowly subsided over time. But, she also told Seth that even now when she recalls what happened, the feelings of anger and embarrassment are still with her, twenty years later.

Amy's story was genuine. It was intimate. It wasn't sugar-coated or moralistic. It didn't even offer Seth a way to "fix" his problem. It was simple, straightforward, and heartfelt. Amy showed Seth she cared so much about him, she was willing to let him see a vulnerable and somewhat unflattering side of herself. Her story not only offered Seth some comfort, it was another piece of her legacy to him. She gave him a glimpse of her own life, without shading the truth.

Seth may never give any indication that this story mattered to him. He and his mom probably won't talk about it again. But he won't forget his mother's honesty and openness. This was a real story, the kind that he's likely to remember with fondness when he thinks about his mother twenty, thirty, or even forty years from now.

If They Wanted to Know, They'd Ask

My dad and I learned early in our relationship not to ask each other personal questions. It would be a cold day in hell before I would have broken our unwritten code of silence. I think he felt the same. In effect, we had our own version of a "don't ask, don't tell" policy. He never said and I never asked.

Think of all the reasons your loved ones might not ask you about the What and Why of your life. Here are just a few:

- They're afraid of hurting your feelings by asking a question that could upset you.
- They think you will be angry with them.

- They think you don't want them to know.
- They think they will bother you.
- They simply don't know how to ask the question.
- You have already established your own "don't ask, don't tell" relationship with them.

Don't assume their silence means your loved ones aren't interested in hearing what you have to say. Operate under the assumption that they want to hear stories about your life, but probably won't ask. Indeed, you might find out that when you begin talking, they are ready and willing to listen. But even if you discover that they won't accept what you have to tell them, say it anyway. You fulfill your responsibility when you offer the gift of you. Whether or not your loved ones accept it is out of your control.

You Can Always Find Time to Talk

My son Jeff was a very good football player until he injured his right leg. He ended up with phlebitis in that leg and was in bed for months. It was during his junior year in high school. But the thing is, I had a lot of time with him. We really got to know each other. I really got to know what his interests and talents were. I didn't do that as much with his brother and sister. I just didn't have the time with them. And the opportunity didn't present itself.

You and your loved ones probably won't have "months" of concentrated time to get to know each other like Jane and her son Jeff did. This is particularly true for those of you who are still raising your children. You'll have to carve out time—a few minutes here and there—from the comings and goings of daily life. But it won't be as difficult as you might initially think. As busy as you are, you probably have a number of opportunities every day to share the What and Why of your life with those you love. Here are some times during the hectic pace of a typical day that you might seize an opening to give another piece of your legacy to those you love the most.

Mealtime. Eating together provides a perfect opportunity to tell a story about yourself. Where you eat your meals together matters much less than starting the conversation. If you eat lunch together on Saturday afternoon at Taco Bell after your daughter's soccer match or at a regularly-scheduled family dinner every Wednesday at the local Italian restaurant, take advantage of the opportunity to share a piece of the What and Why of your life.

Jay and Marilyn told me that whenever their family is together for dinner, wherever that might be, each child has a chance to say what happened during his or her day. That's a wonderful tradition to foster. It could become an even better one if Jay and Marilyn make it a point to include themselves in the discussion.

Drivetime. Parents spend hours rushing their kids from event to event in the car. That's the way we live today. What a great time to transform a high-anxiety chore into an opportunity to talk about yourself. You have a captive audience! Turn off the radio or CD player, forget about the traffic, and tell them something about your life.

I was a chronic complainer in the car while rushing my kids to golf practice, a birthday party, or work after school. I spent the time telling my kids that we were going to be late, there must be a ten-car pileup ahead that we'd never get past, the person in front of us couldn't possibly have passed his driver's test, and on and on. Maybe that's why my kids seemed so anxious to jump out of the car when we finally arrived at our destination. They didn't want to hear anymore complaining from me.

Now I try to give one What or Why about myself during most drive times with my kids. I might tell them why I drive slower than I used to, or why I allow myself more time to get where we are going. I might even retell my ten-year-old's favorite story about the night I hit a deer on a country road and had to hitchhike back to the campus during my freshman year in college. Thomas loves to ask me questions about the night I tangled with the deer. "What did you do with the deer, Dad?" "So you had to walk all the way back to school by yourself in the middle of the night?" "Were you scared?" His eyes get bigger by the second, no matter how many times I retell the story of the blue '65 Chevy and the big buck that suddenly leaped out of the bushes!

Based on my kids' reactions, I've compiled a "top ten stories of my life" that I periodically revisit. Even my three teenagers seem to prefer almost any story about myself over my endless complaints about the traffic. And I like telling my stories. Occasionally, I look forward to the drive, even during rush hour, because I am eager to tell them something else about myself. It's a great way to turn a typically silent and mindless ride into a lively discussion.

Hanging-Around-Together Time. Let's face it. Not many of us watch the marching band at halftime during a football game. So, when your loved ones are with you, turn down the sound on the TV and take a few minutes to share a What or Why about yourself. Maybe tell your daughter why sports are such an important part of your life, or tell her about the time you tried out for the high-school baseball team and ended up as the last player cut from the squad.

Think of all the times you are with a loved one doing yard work, watching TV, or shopping at a store and someone or something triggers a memory of an event from your past. Maybe you are walking through a crowded mall with your teenage son when you pass someone who reminds you of your favorite English teacher in high school, the first person who recognized and nurtured your budding writing talents. When that happens, instead of reminiscing in silence like you normally do, share it with your son. Seize the opportunity. Turn a few seconds of hanging-around-together time into a purposeful gift by giving your loved one a glimpse into your life that you typically would have kept to yourself.

Bedtime. Many of you read bedtime stories to your children. Some parents told me they still read to their young teenagers. How wonderful! Once in a while, replace Dr. Seuss, Harry Potter, or whatever else you are reading that night with a story about yourself. Try making yourself the main event. Or maybe tell a story about yourself that adds a little color to the one you are reading.

I read my youngest son a biography of my boyhood idol, Mickey Mantle. It took us two weeks to finish the book. After each night's reading, I'd talk a little more about my undying allegiance as a child to the New York Yankees. One of my clearest memories of childhood is the day I reverently glued the black-and-white photographs of each of my Yankee heroes into a homemade baseball scrapbook. I liked telling those stories of some happy memories from my youth, and my youngest son seemed to like hearing them.

One night, I even got a chance to bring my parents into my story. My mom and dad were both avid baseball fans. When I was a young boy, on most summer nights we would sit together in the living room watching the Yankee games on New York City's WPIX. It was one of the few things we did together as a family that I remember with fondness. Reading the biography of Mickey Mantle provided a perfect segue into a father-son talk about the influence of baseball on my life as a child and even on my relationship with my parents.

When the opportunity arises to tell a story about yourself, take advantage of it. Written autobiographies, videos, and tape recordings about your life are wonderful ways to teach your loved ones more about you. However, they usually require a considerable amount of time and effort to create. Maybe you don't like to write, or maybe you're a technophobe like me and dread the thought of operating a video camera because you know that the second you turn it on it will stop working. Maybe you are just too busy to even think about these more elaborate and time-consuming ways of sharing your life with those you love. Take the path of least resistance. In this case, it's also the most direct and productive path, because whenever you are together and have a story or a thought about yourself you want to share, all you have to do is talk.

So, stop procrastinating. Forget the excuse that you'll get around to it later. As the TV ad for athletic gear exhorts, "Just do it!"

7

It's Yours to Give

Give It, Don't Leave It

> My legacy? Ugh! It's too far away to think about. At least I hope it is!

When we think about our own legacy, our initial reaction might be similar to Nancy's "Ugh!" To most of us, the word "legacy" signifies a dispersal of our belongings after we are gone. The prevailing notion is that at the point our legacy begins, our own life has ended! So, it's not surprising that we don't think more, or even at all, about our legacy. In fact, most of us hope, like Nancy does, that "it's too far away to think about."

Before you start giving the gift of you to your loved ones, rethink what the essence of the word "legacy" really is. Don't think of it as a "leaving behind" of the wealth you accumulate before you die, but a giving of yourself as your life unfolds. You might leave behind your money and possessions. But you give the most important part of your legacy—the gift of you—today, tomorrow, and every day for the rest of your life!

What If They Want Something Else

I told my son George how much money I have in my savings account. It's only about $5,000. If I gave him all of it, it would not put him where he wants to be. And that's the only money I have other than my pension plan at work. I have never been interested in making a lot of money. I'm sixty-five now and I'm still working. But that's okay, because I like what I do. That's the way I've lived my life. Career advancement was never a big deal for me. Doing what made me happy was important.

So, as far as a legacy goes, it won't be that much financially. It will not be anything that makes George very happy, I can tell you that. If I died today, maybe he would be able to pay off his college loan or something small like that. There is this disappointment on his part, I think, that I don't help him out more. When I visit him, we don't sit and chat like a father and son should do. I am usually driving up there to give him something, like recently when I brought him some furniture. It wasn't new furniture, but it was still in good condition. He didn't seem too excited when he saw it. It's hard to have that kind of relationship with him and not overextend myself or do more than I really think is right.

Mike feels that his thirty-year-old son's interest in him can be summed up in four words: "Show me the money!" They don't "sit and chat" when Mike makes the eighty-mile drive up I-25 to his son's home. He takes something of monetary value—living room furniture, for example—spends a few awkward minutes with his son, daughter-in-law, and grandchildren, and then returns home. Mike is resigned to the notion that his legacy won't amount to much because he doesn't have enough of the one thing George seems to want from him: money.

Mike doesn't believe his legacy consists of the balance in his savings account. He said that honesty, integrity, and perseverance in the face of adversity, values that he feels have guided his life, are what he tried to instill in George. But the message his son seems to give him is a simple and stark one: "The significance of your legacy to me is directly proportionate to the amount of money I receive from you." Sadly, Mike has started to measure his legacy in the same way George does. Thus, he says dejectedly, "If I died today, maybe he would be able to pay off his college loan or something small like that." Right now, Mike is not in control of his own legacy. He doesn't define what it is. George does. And George makes it clear that it's all about money. So Mike does the best he can, knowing he is fighting a losing battle. He will never meet his son's expectations, although he continues to try by giving him gifts and small sums of money and, as he said, doing "more than I really think is right."

Be careful not to let others define your legacy. It's not only yours to give, it's yours to define. But it's easy to let others define it for you. Maybe it feels like your daughter's main interest in you is making sure she is in line to take over your business when you die. Maybe your son and daughter-in-law subtly lobby for your summer home in the mountains every time they visit. Or maybe your spouse wants a written assurance that if she dies before you, her children by a first marriage will inherit some of your money. Or, as Mike speculates when trying to understand his son's sense of entitlement to his money, maybe an ex-spouse tells the children that you are not giving them their fair share of your assets.

You might even let people outside of your family define your legacy for you. The "experts" bombard you with warnings that if you haven't executed the proper estate-planning documents, the taxman can inherit more of your assets than your own family! And they are absolutely correct. By following their advice, you might save your loved ones many thousands of dollars and a lot of unnecessary heartache after you are gone. But virtually all the warnings, urgings, and advice reinforce the notion that your legacy is nothing more than your money and possessions. You don't read advertisements in your local newspaper urging you to attend estate-planning seminars on the best ways to give the gift of you to your loved ones. No, all the fuss and focus is on what matters the least, your money and things.

You can properly execute your will, trust, Letter of Last Instructions, or any other legal document you wish and still make sure your loved ones realize that, although you are willing to spend the time and money it takes to assure that all your worldly goods get to the right people after you are gone, *you are not the sum of your stuff.* Let them know that you have a much more important legacy than money to give them. And that they won't have to wait until you are dead and buried to receive it. Show them that by talking about yourself and sharing stories about your life, you are determined to give them their most important legacy starting right now and for the rest of your lives together. Teach them that the most precious gift you have to give them, the people you love the most, is you!

Can you imagine how much better you'll feel? And how much better off your loved ones will be, even if they don't think so or realize it at the time?

Give It Unconditionally

Lets revisit Mike's relationship with his son George, whose primary interest seems to be his father's money. Earlier in the book, I suggested that starting with a simple and nonthreatening What or Why gradually allows those standing at the bottom of the ladder to build a tolerance for intimate conversation with you.

But Mike's son isn't standing passively below the ladder waiting to hear his dad speak. He's shaking the ladder his dad is standing on! He wants to know where the money is. He's damn mad. He and his father have a relationship that is hurtling toward a total and irreversible estrangement. Mike doesn't have the luxury of slowly and cautiously testing George's reaction to his thoughts. Time is rapidly running out. He has to move quickly and forcefully down the ladder toward his son. Here's one of many ways Mike might begin the process of doing so:

> Son, I need to talk with you. . . .

> I'm worried about our relationship. It seems that all we talk about is money. You seem upset that I don't help you enough with your financial needs. Then I become defensive and resentful. . . .

> I want us to have a better relationship. I hope you too. I'm afraid that if we continue like we are now, our relationship will be ruined. . . .

> *I want you to know* that I've never been interested in making a lot of money. *It's been more important to me* to have a job I like, even if it didn't pay much. So, I don't have a lot of money now. I don't regret it—I've enjoyed my life. . . .

Continued

I think it's important that I tell you where things stand for me now. I'm sixty-five years old and getting ready to retire. I don't have money to give you. I need what I have saved for my retirement years. . . .

I hope you can accept that. And I hope you and I can learn to enjoy each other's company more than we have in the past. I love you. I want us to be closer. . . .

We have never talked much, and it might be hard to start now. But my relationship with you is too important to me to let arguments about money ruin it. . . .

I want you to know me better, Son, and I want to know you better. I'm ready to let you know more about who I am and what is important to me. And why I live life the way I do. . . .

I think those are the kinds of things I should give you now. When I die, any money left over will go to you. But now, while we are still together, I want to enjoy being with you. . . .

I've never been good at talking about myself or about the two of us. I can't change the past. But I am ready to go forward and try to build a better relationship with you.

Will this bold attempt by Mike to connect with his son begin to repair their relationship? Maybe not. It's hard to imagine Mike's thirty-year-old son replacing his lust for money with a passion for stories about his dad's life. Any attempt by Mike to substitute himself for his checkbook at this point is likely to be quickly rejected by George. Mike faces a long and difficult road ahead if he tries to shift the focus of his relationship with his son from money to the What and Why of his life.

When Mike begins to talk about himself—to bare his soul and make himself vulnerable—what if George walks away from him? Or what if he says, "Look, Dad, I'm not interested," or, "Dad, it's too late to start talking about that now." What will happen if each time Mike tries to talk about his life with his son, George responds with more questions about the money? Mike will probably have to try repeatedly, in different ways, in different places, and at different times, to talk about himself with his son. Ultimately, he may get nothing back from George but a cold shoulder and more questions about his checkbook. Why should he expose himself to the hurt and humiliation?

As difficult as it might be, Mike must give the gift of himself unconditionally, which means with absolutely no strings attached. The value of his gift emanates from the giving of it, not from his son's reaction to it or from what Mike hopes to receive in return—a more meaningful relationship with his son. This is a critical point to understand.

Whether George treats the gift like the one thing he has always dreamed of having, or like another piece of used living-room furniture he never really wanted in the first place, neither enhances nor diminishes the importance of what Mike is offering him. The significance of Mike's gift emanates from his willingness to give himself to his son. He is allowing

George an opportunity to see and understand the essence of who he is as a man and a father. Furthermore, he is giving his gift without requiring anything in return, not even a simple "thank you" from his son. So, as senseless as it might seem for Mike to risk more hurt and embarrassment, it is exactly this vulnerability to which he is exposing himself that makes his gift such a special one.

Don't Give It by Default

> My legacy . . . Well, it's pretty simple. I die. Then Peggy dies, and the kids get the money and whatever else we own.

Dave, a retired accountant, is angry and disgusted with his two grown children, both of whom live in the same town as their parents. They rarely show any concern at all for him or their mother, Peggy. He and Peggy will soon celebrate their fiftieth wedding anniversary. They are both convinced their children won't even remember, let alone plan a celebration for them. Dave describes his daughter as a "chronic complainer" and his son as a "constant taker." He and Peggy live in a persistent state of tension with their children. Dave shakes his head and says, "We wonder where we went wrong."

Dave's blunt assessment of his legacy is shortsighted. Yes, after he and Peggy die, according to their wills, "the kids get the money." However, they have already gotten much more than that. He has already given them all the good and bad times they had together, everything they saw him do, whether they understood it or not, and all that was said and left unsaid. No, Dave's legacy is not as simple as he thinks it is.

Dave sees his legacy in much the same way a passenger on a ship views an iceberg. Just the tip, perhaps one-tenth of the whole, is clearly visible. The remaining 90 percent stays out of sight. The 10 percent Dave sees is his money and possessions. He thinks his legacy consists of only the tangible things that can be listed, assessed, and divided after his death. The unseen 90 percent, the real core of his legacy, he has been giving to his family as they live their lives together. He has been giving his legacy to his children for more than forty years, although he has done so unconsciously and without purpose. Sadly, he has been giving his legacy by default.

What should Dave do? He is seventy-two years old. Time is growing short. He needs to begin telling his children who he is and what kind of relationship he wants with them. Here's an idea how he could start. Right now, he is bracing himself for yet another disappointment. He believes that his children won't even remember his fiftieth wedding anniversary, let alone plan a celebration. Based on their previous track record, his prediction will probably become a reality. They'll forget about the anniversary and then he'll become even more disenchanted with and disconnected from his son and daughter. Why not make sure they don't forget? Why not remind them? Why not even go one step further and ask them to help plan a celebration? He and Peggy can spearhead the planning and either or both of the children can help with some of the details. What a wonderful opportunity for the four of them to break the cycle of negative interactions.

Would he and Peggy be setting themselves up for one more disappointment? Maybe. But why not risk it? Right now, the relationship with their children, like Mike's with his son, is on life support. Why not turn the upcoming anniversary into a first step toward mending their relationship instead of passively allowing it to become one more piece of evidence that somewhere, as Dave lamented, "we went wrong." Indeed, he may ask for help and they may both say no. But maybe one or both of them will agree and follow through, and maybe he'll have found a jumping-off point to reconnect with his children. Maybe they'll plan as a family, he'll finally have a chance to thank them for something they've done, and perhaps even find openings during this extremely rare positive interaction to move closer to his children by sharing some of his thoughts and feelings with them.

For those of you who identify with Dave's and Mike's emotionally grinding relationships with their children, maybe it's time for you to try to turn the next interaction with your loved ones from another disappointment into a first step toward reconnecting with them. The visible tip of your legacy might be your money and possessions. But you or a paid professional can easily create a detailed list specifying who gets each item after you are gone. That will take care of the small and relatively insignificant piece of what you have to give them.

Start distributing the core of your legacy by engaging in a conscious and ongoing giving of the What and Why of your life. Stop allowing the 10 percent to masquerade as the sum of your legacy, while the heart of it—the unspoken 90 percent—continues to be a legacy by default. Don't let your predictions that your loves ones will continue to disappoint you become self-fulfilling simply because you are already convinced it's pointless trying to become more emotionally connected to them. And remember that when all is said and done, even if your loved ones reject every attempt you make to tell them who you really are, recognize the significance of what you have tried to do. You have offered them your most priceless legacy, the gift of you!

Don't Give It by Proxy

> We didn't talk much as a family when I was a kid. I really don't talk that much with Gary. That has always been more of Sharon's role as his mother. When you think about it, it makes sense. I was working and Sharon was with Gary all day, so they developed a better relationship. He and his mother can talk.

It's easy and convenient to let someone else take care of the parts of life we aren't comfortable dealing with, such as discussing emotional matters with a loved one. Sharon takes care of this for her husband, Ken. As Ken recalled, his mother took care of it for his father.

Often, one parent, usually the mother, becomes spokesperson for the spouse when personal matters, including the What and Why of the silent parent's life, are discussed with children. My mother told me most of what I learned about my father's life. Years after Dad died, my mom would occasionally say, "Bill, did you know your father liked to . . . ?" or, "Bill, did you know that your dad . . . ?" I learned more about my father during the last couple of years of my mother's life than I did during the twenty-five years he and I were together.

I found out from my mom that Dad was a championship swimmer when he was a teenager. One day she opened the antique cedar chest in her bedroom, searched under a stack of heavy woolen blankets, and lifted out an old brown shoebox. Three small, badly tarnished trophies were inside the box. Each was loosely wrapped in tissue paper. The trophies were so old that the inscriptions on two of them were unreadable. The inscription on the third "loving cup" as my mom called it, read:

1st Place
YMCA Swim Meet
Poughkeepsie, New York
May 3rd, 1916

Mom handed the trophies to me and said, "Your dad was proud of these, although he would never admit it." Until that day when my mother opened the cedar chest, I didn't know the three trophies existed, let alone that they might have been important to my father.

As we sat together looking at the trophies, my mother asked, "Did you know your dad was a master carpenter?" I didn't. We went downstairs to the living room where she pointed out two bookcases and a magazine rack that Dad had designed and built when he was in his forties, several years before I was born. I had grown up using these pieces of furniture every day for almost twenty years, never knowing that my dad had made them. As grateful as I am that my mother helped me to better know my dad, it wasn't her job to tell me. It was my dad's responsibility. It's not Sharon's duty to let Gary know who his dad really is. Ken needs to do it himself. It's not your spouse's responsibility to tell your loved ones the What and Why of your life. It's yours. It's your legacy to give. Don't leave it to your spouse or anyone else to fill in the blanks about your life. A secondhand transfer of the stories of your life is not a substitute for you sharing them with the people you love. When you give the gift of you, your loved ones know *you* want them to have it. When your spouse does it for you, your loved ones are only sure that *he* or *she* wanted you to have it. Don't give the What and Why of your life by proxy. Give them directly. Let your loved ones know beyond any doubt that the stories of your life have too much importance to be shared by anyone other than you!

Start with Your Legacy

Start by talking about yourself. Make sure your loved ones know who *you* are before you try to tell them who you and your spouse are together. Much of what matters to you and why you live life the way you do is unique to you. Your spouse has his or her own stories to share. Your loved ones know that. They know that both of you don't view life in exactly the same way. Help them to better understand the difference in perspectives by hearing from each of you about your own lives.

My dad and mom came from different backgrounds. They had different life experiences. They seemed to share many beliefs and values. Others they didn't share, like my mother's strong religious convictions. For me to gain insight into their lives together, I needed to know more about each of them as individuals. Your joint legacy will take on much more meaning for your loved ones if you are each able to talk about yourself first. I can imagine my mom saying, "Bill, your dad and I want to tell you what we think is important in life," and my dad quickly saying, "OK, Gertrude, you take it from here,

I've got some painting to finish!" He probably would have dashed right back up his ladder, safe again on the top rung. It just wouldn't have worked. If my mom said it for both of them, even if my dad stood there while she did, I wouldn't be convinced it was what he too *really* thought.

Tell your kids who *you* are. Let your spouse tell them who he or she is. Even if your spouse doesn't want to or can't seem to do it, you lead the way. After seeing and hearing you share the What and Why of your life, your spouse might be ready to begin.

8

What Will Really Change?

When he was in the hospital, I just hated going there and seeing him like that. As soon as the hospital was in sight, my stomach started to churn. And then that hospital smell as soon as you walk in. . . . Worst of all was going into his room three or four times a day and seeing him laying in bed with all the machines and tubes and all the noise. God, I just hated seeing him like that. That's not the father I knew. Then one day he whispered to me, "Rose Marie, I'm dying. I need to talk with you. I've got some things I need to tell you." And I said, "Dad, don't talk like that. I don't like to hear you say that." I kept putting him off. I didn't want to deal with the fact that there was going to be an end—that he was really going to die. He kept trying to talk to me because he knew he was dying, and honest-to-God, I just felt like screaming and running out of the room. I just couldn't listen to him talk about that. Now I regret it. I should have let him talk.

Listening, Even When It Hurts

Rose Marie's father wanted to talk. Al knew he was short on time. With only a few days left, he uttered a desperate plea to his only child: "Rose Marie, I'm dying. I need to talk with you." Rose Marie could not listen. She couldn't face her father's death. During our interview she reminisced about the love and admiration she had for her father, a penniless immigrant from Russia who became a successful and respected Seattle businessman. She proudly described him as someone "always able to make the tough decisions." She just couldn't imagine life without her beloved father. But as we talked, there seemed to be another reason Rose Marie avoided that deathbed conversation with her father.

As much as she loved her dad, Rose Marie had almost no experience talking with him about anything personal. She remembered story after story about trying to get her dad to "tell me what he was thinking about. He just couldn't or wouldn't do it. Every day he would charge forward making decisions about his business, and it was almost like he couldn't slow down and spend any time with us just being himself. He was a high-control person. It just didn't seem to be in his nature to let us in his little world."

Al never talked about himself with Rose Marie. He wouldn't talk about his two years in combat during World War II. When Rose Marie asked about it, he would tell her it was "too gruesome and horrible" to discuss. He wouldn't talk with her about life as a boy in Russia. He used to say, "That's not something I want to remember." He wouldn't talk with her about his work—a maze of commercial and residential rental properties. He would tell her that after he died, "This will all be yours." But whenever she asked him to show her what he did each day and what he expected her to do with the business after he was gone, he would say, "Not now. It's too complicated. We'll talk about it later."

The day finally came when Al realized that there was no time left. This was "later." He tried to rush down his ladder on his deathbed, but Rose Marie couldn't deal with the sudden burst of emotion and intimacy. Much to her deep regret, she ran the other way. Al wanted to talk, but Rose Marie simply couldn't listen. It was her turn to say, in effect, "Not now. We'll talk about it later."

A few months after my mother suffered a heart attack, she repeatedly tried to talk to me about the reality of her advancing age and deteriorating health. She would say, "Bill, I want to talk to you about my will and . . ." I wouldn't even let her get all of the words out of her mouth. I cut her off with my standard response: "Mom, you're not going anywhere. We've got plenty of time for that." After a few attempts and subsequent rebuffs by me, she stopped trying to get me to listen. I was relieved at the time, but almost twenty years later, I still feel guilty that I refused to let her talk.

I didn't want to discuss it for much the same reason Rose Marie avoided that deathbed talk with her father. I didn't want to face my mother's death. But that's only one of the reasons. My mother and I, like Rose Marie and her dad, didn't talk about ourselves with each other. Never! So when she felt the need to talk, her sense of urgency couldn't compete with my overwhelming discomfort. Discussions like this were simply outside the boundaries of our relationship. I wasn't ready or willing to suddenly redefine those boundaries, especially when it involved talking about such a deeply emotional and intimate subject—the end of my mother's life.

Elderly parents told similar stories throughout our interviews. Barbara, for example, hopes that her daughter Jo Ann "won't put me away someplace . . . in one of those nursing homes. . . . I had a mild heart attack a few months ago, so wondering about where I'm going to end up is on my mind now." But Barbara has never told any of this to her daughter because she "doesn't want to upset her. Jo Ann has her own problems to worry about." So Barbara lives with her ever-increasing fear of nursing homes and the hope that "Jo Ann will know what to do when the time comes."

Brad, a retired teacher, has never talked to his kids about what he expects from them if he becomes unable to take care of himself. "What will they do?" he asked himself out loud. "I don't know. . . . I guess they will do whatever they can."

Ruth, a seventy-one-year-old mother of three children, said, "The time we [she and her husband Sam] have left is limited. We need to start talking to the kids more, and very soon, about our final wishes. But they just don't like to think about that kind of stuff."

No, we don't like thinking about that kind of stuff. We like talking about it even less, especially after a lifetime of standing at opposite ends of the ladder. How can urgent pleas of "we have to talk" overcome the effects of a lifetime of little or no intimate communication? They usually don't. People who know the end is near and desperately want to talk watch their loved ones pull away. Often, they die in silence, and the people who survive them spend the rest of their lives wishing they had been able to listen.

Don't let this happen to you or your loved ones. When you honestly and openly say, "Here's who I am. Here's what matters to me. Here's why I live my life the way I do," you gradually teach your loved ones how to feel comfortable having a personal and intimate conversation with you. Over time, you'll both be ready to tackle even the most sensitive and emotionally charged subjects. Those of you who want to talk about your fear of nursing homes, or at what point you want the doctor to turn off the life-support equipment, or how you want your final wishes carried out will be able to do so without having your adult children run the other way. Those of you with younger children will create a less threatening environment for parent-child discussions about those most dreaded of all subjects—sex, drugs, and alcohol. As you learn to talk, they'll learn to listen, even when the subject matter isn't particularly pleasant. Even when it hurts.

Putting the "Stuff" in Its Place

My brother is still upset about what he got when Dad died. He keeps threatening to hire a lawyer because he thinks I took more than I was entitled to. It's just ridiculous. I mean, my dad's total estate amounted to about $20,000 in bank accounts and his house that we sold for $70,000. I got half of the proceeds and my brother got the other half. Now don't get me wrong, I was glad to get it. But I wish my dad would have spent his money on himself. My brother seems convinced he got shortchanged. I've given him a complete accounting of the estate and he still complains. It's pathetic. He and my dad never got along. He hadn't visited Dad for years, even when he was sick. Whatever he got is probably more than he deserved.

Maybe these words are nothing more than an expression of one brother's contempt for another. After all, family feuds that simmer for years are often ignited by the death of a parent. It's possible that Richard's recollection of an ungrateful and greedy brother stems from a long-standing feud with his sibling. But even if this is the case, Richard's description of his brother's behavior clearly reflects a family dynamic I witnessed countless times in my financial-planning practice when I assisted in the dispersal of a deceased parent's assets.

I saw that those who were the most estranged from the deceased person seemed to have the most interest in the size of their inheritance. Those who had the best relationship were likely to have the least interest in "how much" their inheritance was worth. They didn't want to talk about the money.

They wanted to talk about how much they missed their mother or father. They were happy with mementos that had little monetary value, perhaps the old living-room clock they watched their mother wind each day or their father's favorite coffee cup—whatever reminded them of the time they spent with their loved one. Unhappy family members, such as Richard's brother, are much more likely to show up with a calculator in hand when the assets are divided. They want as much as they can possibly get.

The more a relationship seems devoid of intimacy, the more the money and possessions seem to matter to the surviving family member. Richard might carry his father's pocket watch because it's a constant reminder of his relationship with his father. His brother might want it because it adds to the bottom line of his inheritance. He might not see any way to measure his dad's feelings for him other than to compare the value of Richard's inheritance with his own.

We shouldn't be surprised to hear stories of family members squabbling over the assets of parents from whom they were emotionally disconnected. I witnessed family infighting on many occasions when people arrived at my office to claim their inheritances. In relationships lacking intimacy, emotion, and openness, many assumed, "if Mom left more stuff to you, isn't it reasonable for me to conclude that she liked you better than me?" Money and possessions can seem like the only tools available to evaluate a disconnected relationship. The most important part of the relationship, much like the 90 percent of an iceberg submerged below the water line, didn't show itself during life. The 10 percent that was in sight all those years spent together—the money and the other stuff—continue to define the relationship, even after death.

My aunt recently died just six months before her hundredth birthday. In her will she left me a rather ornate, antique, five-legged chair made from cherry wood. For forty years she reminded me that when she died, the chair was mine. I didn't care about the chair when I was ten years old and I don't care about it now. The chair has no meaning for me because I was never connected to my aunt. Even though I saw her frequently, I never really got to know her. Her life was a mystery to me. The truth is, I would have gone to the trouble and expense of having the chair shipped from the East Coast to my home in Colorado only if it had enough monetary value. Otherwise, it wasn't worth it to me; it had absolutely no emotional value for me. After an estate tax appraisal valued it at a couple of hundred dollars, I decided that it didn't make good financial sense to have it shipped across the country. So, I donated it to the Salvation Army in the city in which my aunt lived.

If my aunt and I had had a meaningful relationship and she had said to me something like: "Bill, I have picked out this chair just for you. When I die, I want you to have it. I hope it will remind you of me and our time together," I would have done whatever it took to get that chair, whether it was worth a thousand dollars or ten cents. In that case, the chair would have been a lasting reminder of our relationship.

The bottom line is this: unless you learn to give the gift of you to your loved ones while you are together, they may be left behind measuring your legacy in terms of dollars and cents and fighting with one another while they are each calculating the value of their piece of the pie. If you demonstrate that your real legacy to them is the What and Why of your life, they will be much more able to see your money and possessions for what they really are—an expression of your affection for them. When you give them the gift of yourself, *you* will matter the most to the people you love, and all the stuff will follow in its proper place. It sounds like the basis for a healthy and happy relationship from cradle to grave, doesn't it?

Heading Off the Regrets

Nobody, in the final moments of this life, will look back and say, "Gee, I should have spent more time working," or "I should have had a bigger bank account!" I know I won't. My regret is that I didn't spend more time with the kids. But back then, I didn't think like that. I wish I had taken that hike up Pikes Peak with them to see a sunset or do some of the other things we talked about doing but never did. You know, the things that are really important.

Harry, a sixty-eight-year-old retired sign painter, echoed the feelings of most fathers of adult children. They too regretted not spending more time with their loved ones. Stan, a prominent businessman and community leader said, "If I had it to do over, I would put more investment in my children and less in myself." Jack, a retired attorney, simply said, "I wasn't home as much as I probably should have been." Paul, a railroad worker for forty years, was the most direct when expressing his regrets. He looked at his wife sitting beside him and said, "I'm sorry I wasn't there. I really missed out."

Many of the women I interviewed were stay-at-home mothers who regretted spending too much time running the household and not enough time getting to know their children. They were usually more specific about their regrets than the men. Roberta, for example, said, "I wish we would have had more discussions with the kids about where each of them was going in life."

Maureen was even more specific, remembering, "I didn't realize as a young parent the influence I had on the children. It wasn't until they were grown with children of their own that one of them said she always wondered why I quit my secretarial job. And one of my sons wondered why I read so much and listened to so much classical music [laughs]. I don't think you realize the effect you have on them until it's too late."

Maybe that's why so many older parents cherish the time they spend with their grandchildren. Jean mused, "Most people think grandparents like to be with their grandkids because we can spoil them and then send them back home to their parents! I think maybe grandkids give a lot of us a second chance. We can spend time with them and pay attention to them in a way we might not have done with their parents." Or, as Paul said, "Every day with the grandkids is like a bonus. I wish I had had as much fun with my kids as I do with my grandkids."

If you are a young parent still raising children, heed the advice of the real experts—the generation that raised you. Spend more time being with and talking to your children. Don't wait until you have grandkids to experience the feeling of closeness you want with your own children. You have the luxury of time that your older counterparts no longer have. Start with your own children while they are young and the most eager and open to listen and learn about who you really are.

Consider the advice of Nina, a sixty-four-year-old administrative assistant who raised two children on her own. She said:

If I could hope for one thing for young parents, it would be that they could see the impact they have on their kids right now. Not just as they look back in their later years.

Older parents, don't live passively with your regrets. Don't assume it's too late. Don't wallow in the misery of empty speculation about "where you went wrong" with your children. Whether your children are thirty, forty, fifty, or sixty years old, most of them will never lose their hunger for knowing who you are, *even though they never say so.* Whether you live another month, year, decade, or longer, if you begin telling your children who you really are by sharing what matters to you and why you live life the way you do, you nurture the possibility that these essential conversations can lead to a more meaningful relationship.

Those of you without children, give your legacy to others you love. Don't believe for a second that the stories of your life have no meaning because you have no children with whom to share them. Give them to the niece who loves you like a mother. Or give them to the children in your classroom who have become the focus of your life. Or give them to the brother, sister, godchild, or friend who lives a thousand miles away but never stops missing you. Let them know who you are: You, who love them so much and, in turn, mean more to them than you will probably ever know!

9

It's Yours for the Asking

You have me thinking about my older sister, Joan. She lives back on the East Coast. I only hear from her at Christmas, when we exchange cards through the mail. We never really have gotten to know each other. The last time we were together was at our mother's funeral ten years ago. I think it's because there is such an age difference between us. Joan was twenty-one when she got married and moved to Bridgeport. I had just turned six! So, I really don't remember living with her except for some vague memories. In my mind's eye I can see her as a teenager, sitting on the front porch reading paperback novels and eating vanilla ice cream [laughs]. That's about it. But you know, I think she is a neat person. My sister Bonnie, who is a few years younger than Joan, has kind of filled me in on Joan's life over the years. Before I was born, she apparently had some pretty serious emotional problems. The story is that she had to be put in a psychiatric facility because of what we would call depression today. Apparently she fought it on and off all of her life. But she raised a nice family of seven kids and became a state leader in the fight for the rights of the handicapped, I think because our younger sister has a disability. I do remember her as bright, pretty, and very well-spoken. She used to lobby at the state legislature. Not bad for someone who never went to college. She has the least education of any of us kids and she probably is the smartest of us all.

Anyway, for some reason, I've been thinking about her lately. Maybe because we are all getting older in a hurry. Every time I get a card from her, I regret not knowing her better. I'd still like to get to know her. But, it would seem awkward to approach her now after all these years. What would I say? "Joan, I'd like to get to know you better"? It just seems too weird to start saying that now. I mean, how would I even go about it? Oh well, it's probably too late in the game to even worry about it.

—Tom, forty-two, single, and brother to three sisters

Like Tom, many of the people I interviewed said that our discussions about life and legacy made them realize that they needed to share more of their lives with loved ones, and they could identify a sister, brother, uncle, grandparent, in-law, or someone else close to them about whom they wanted to know more. But like Tom, while we wish for better communication, we often resign ourselves to a lament that "it's probably too late." Or, like Fred, who has an older brother he hasn't seen or talked with in eight years, we too might say, "Oh well, no sense making anyone feel uncomfortable after all these years." Or, like Todd, when talking about his brother, we might use this convenient excuse to remain disconnected: "Oh well, if we didn't live so far apart from each other, it might have turned out differently." Or, as Ted said about his favorite uncle, "Oh well, I just don't think people of their generation like to talk about themselves and I guess I have to respect that." These "oh wells" might seem harmless, but they have an insidious effect on our lives. They perpetuate our disconnection from people we care about by discouraging us from trying to have closer relationships with them.

As we discussed previously, we keep our questions to ourselves because we don't want to upset our loved ones, seem like we are prying into their private lives, violate the unwritten "don't ask, don't tell" policy that might have ruled our relationship for years, or simply be a bother to them. It can seem safer and more prudent to say "oh well" and walk away with our questions still unanswered than to risk creating discomfort for them or us. It might even seem smarter to have no relationship at all than an uncomfortable one. But your desire to know your loved ones better or to reconnect with them won't diminish with time. In fact, it will probably grow stronger, as will your disappointment in yourself that you still haven't begun asking your questions.

Turning "Oh Well" into "Ah Yes"

When I grew up, we had this small, oval-shaped mahogany table in the living room right by the front window. It had a pullout drawer with a silver handle. The drawer was stuffed with old photographs. Every so often, I'd pull out a handful of those pictures and look through them. Some were pictures of my brother and sister and me that I recognized right away. But honestly, I'll bet I couldn't identify half of the people in those pictures. My brother and sister weren't much help. They might have been able to identify a few more people than me, but not many. I think we all figured that if it was important for us to know who this person or that person was, Mom would have told us. And the way the pictures were stuffed in the drawer made you think they weren't important anyway.

I had just gotten home for summer break after my junior year in college. I really think I owe what happened next to my college roommate. He was from a real open family. I went to his house that year for a few days during Easter vacation. Holy cow! People in his family hugged and kissed whenever they saw each other! Aunts and uncles and brothers and sisters, it was amazing. One night, his mother gets out these family photo albums and starts showing me pictures of Jack when he was a kid. And pictures of her mother and father. And pictures of Aunt this and Cousin that. Almost every picture had a label under it identifying who the person was and when the picture was taken. I'll never forget it. I had never been around anybody so family-oriented. So, when I went home for the summer, one day I grabbed a bunch of pictures out of the drawer and asked my mother to sit with me a minute and tell me who the people in the pictures were. She gave me that same old response, "Oh, I don't even think I'd remember, most of those pictures are so old." This time, instead of just saying "OK" and letting her walk away, I asked her again to sit down and give it a try. I can remember the surprised look on her face [laughs]. But she finally sat down. You wouldn't have believed it. She started to identify family members I never knew. "This is your dad's grandfather. Here's my father and his brother." And on it went. My gosh, she even showed me pictures of her and Dad in their twenties. I never knew it was them! Here's my dad in one of those 1940s zoot suits, I think they called them [laughs].

Boy, did that open up the floodgates for my mom. The next day we were sitting in the living room and she said, "Phil, did I show you the picture of your Uncle Wilfred, in Germany during World War II?" She goes to the drawer and starts pulling out pictures of her brother. And then the stories started to come. I mean, this may sound like no big deal to you, but it was so out of character for my mom to talk about her family. I can remember it like it was yesterday. All of a sudden she   started to tell me about herself and all these relatives I never knew. It was great. My brother and sister couldn't believe it!

—Phil, fifty-one-year-old engineer and father and grandfather

Let's face it. It's likely that your silent mother, father, or other loved one is having as much trouble talking as you are asking your questions. If the silence is ever going to end, you might have to take it upon yourself to begin the conversation. It might be up to you to break the usual pattern of behavior: they try to talk, you don't respond or somehow show your displeasure, and they become silent again. Or conversely, you ask, they demonstrate their unwillingness to respond—maybe by a familiar look, gesture, or a few words that deter you from asking again—and you retreat into your silence.

As Phil learned to his utter amazement, sometimes it just takes a little extra prodding to get the conversation started. After all those years, he finally broke his mother's silence by gently encouraging her to "give it a try." The first time Phil's mother talked about the pictures in the drawer, she gave him the names of some of the people, but not much more than that. But as Phil said, whenever they revisited the pictures during that summer, "she seemed to think of one more thing to tell me."

Phil was astounded to learn how much impact some of the people in the photos had on his mother's life. He learned about his mother's Aunt Mary, an independent woman who never married and lived alone in a small cottage in the woods of New Hampshire. He discovered that his mother spent almost every summer of her childhood with Aunt Mary, the "original women's libber," as his mom fondly remembered her.

"She taught me to think for myself. Something my mother didn't do. My father did the thinking for both of them." Wow! Phil was astounded by this remarkable revelation about his mother's upbringing. It occurred to him that those summers with Aunt Mary might explain where his mother developed the strong will and sense of self-sufficiency he had seen her demonstrate all his life.

And then one day, his mother identified the man in the thick, cardboardlike photograph as her father. Phil had seen this picture countless times before as he aimlessly sifted through that drawer full of photographs. In fact, he sheepishly admitted that he and his brother found this particular picture to be the perfect shape and weight to sidearm at each other when they were kids. They didn't know they were tossing a picture of Grandpa back and forth!

The dour looking, thirty-something-year-old man sitting stiffly for the camera, dressed in a pinstriped three-piece suit, was his grandfather James, who died eight years before Phil was born. "He was not a very happy man," according to Phil's mother. He remembers her holding the picture and saying, "He died in his early forties from a heart attack. I think he just never liked life very much. I don't know why. But I do know that your dad and I finally decided to move far away from him or I don't think our marriage would have lasted." Wow, another incredible family story that Phil heard for the first time! And this recollection by Phil's mother led to a whole string of stories about the early years of his parents' marriage. His mother told stories about where they lived, how they struggled to get along with her controlling father and his neurotic mother, and how, much to Phil's amazement, his father finally agreed to move to a different state in order to save his marriage from meddling in-laws.

Asking his mother about the pictures just one more time was all it took for Phil to turn the pile of old photos into a rich and meaningful history about forgotten family members and never-before-told family stories.

Where are those pictures today? Occupying a place of honor in Phil's own living room. "I've got them mounted in photo albums. My kids love to hear the stories about all those relatives who died years before any of them were born."

Ah, yes! Now, those unknown faces in the photos have become members of the family, not only for Phil but for also for his children. And they've become real people, through stories about their faults and failings as well as their strengths and accomplishments. It all started with Phil making sure that his mother began sharing her "legacy of the heart," which would have gone to the grave with her when she died three years ago if he simply hadn't kept asking his question.

Here You Come . . . and Up the Ladder They Run

Will you experience the stunning results that Phil did simply by asking your questions? Will you finally start communicating with a parent you thought never liked you, like Jerry did when he finally discovered that his eighty-two-year-old father was worried about him because he stopped attending church forty years ago?

You might be that fortunate. But you are more likely to discover that, although you are willing to begin the dialogue, your loved ones still don't seem ready to talk. Old ways of interacting are not easily changed. If I had looked up from the bottom of the ladder on one of those hot August days and begun asking my dad questions about his father who died before I was born, or why he felt the yearly ritual of scraping and painting could not be skipped just once so we could spend a vacation together, or about anything else that required him to assess and reveal his thoughts and feelings, I would have probably chased him two or three rungs higher! That might be what you end up doing too, when you begin asking a loved one personal questions. Be ready for it. Don't give up after one or two attempts. Don't mutter another "oh well" and walk away. Try again. You've taken that first all-important step toward your loved one by asking your question. The question might prompt an annoyed response like, "Why do you want to know that?" Or, you might find your question quickly dismissed by, "Oh, I really don't remember," or, "It was so long ago. It's really not important anymore." If you are lucky enough to receive a thoughtful and substantive response, enjoy it, but if you hear impatience, avoidance, or even anger in the response of a loved one, don't let it dissuade you from asking again.

Remember that you might be breaking new ground when you ask loved ones to share their private thoughts with you. "Don't ask, don't tell" relationships fade away slowly. Try not to personalize a disappointing response to the question you have waited so long to ask. If you are shaking the ladder for the first time, it can be upsetting to both of you. But also remember that neither of you will be permanently damaged by learning to work through a little face-to-face discomfort with each other. In fact, anticipating that you might both be uncomfortable is an important first step in establishing meaningful communication. Learning to accept the initial feeling of discomfort will help you both avoid using another "oh well" that might give you some short-term relief, but will also continue to perpetuate the silence that rules your relationship.

Make Asking Easy on Both of You

If you are redefining the boundaries of an old relationship by asking questions, make it as easy as possible for you to ask and for your loved ones to respond. If they feel blindsided by a question that seems embarrassing, confrontational, or otherwise difficult to answer, you are both likely to regret that the question was ever asked. Remember Marlene's question to each of her three sons: "What do you think about me?" Each son had a different reaction to that question, but the net result was the same—not one of them felt comfortable answering it. The more your loved ones feel threatened by what you ask, the more likely they are to push you away, causing each of you to say to yourselves, "Don't do that again!"

Here are some ways to make what might be your first foray into the private thoughts of someone you love a successful one or, at the very least, a relatively comfortable interaction for both of you:

- Start with questions that are not emotionally charged. Sometimes, when we finally muster up enough courage to ask a personal question that we have suppressed for years, we blurt out something that instantly puts our loved one on the defensive. The longer the silence has lasted, the safer the question should be. Phil just kept asking this simple question, "Mom, who is the person in this picture?" He didn't say, "Why won't you tell me who this person is?" or, "Why don't you want me to know about my grandfather?" Keep the question and your approach as nonthreatening and as matter-of-fact as you can.

- Start with questions about something your loved ones might enjoy talking about. If I could do it all over again, I might try starting my dad down his ladder by asking about his love of swimming as a young man or the amazing collection of tools he had meticulously and methodically hung on the basement wall. Queries about your loved ones' hobbies or personal accomplishments are a perfect jumping-off point for you to gain confidence asking your questions and for them to learn how to respond.

- Be patient. Remember that it takes time to learn how to talk with and about each other. At first, you may feel yourself expending an inordinate amount of effort and energy trying to ask very simple questions. Over time, your questions and their responses will become much more substantive with much less effort. It just takes time.

- Try to choose the best time and place to ask your question. Thanksgiving dinner with all the relatives around the table might not be the opportune time to ask your quiet bachelor Uncle Hal if he ever regrets not having children of his own. Save that one for a private time together. People who are not used to talking about themselves respond better to safe questions asked in safe settings. In the beginning, they might struggle to answer the simplest of questions, especially if they are worrying about what bystanders (especially other family members) are thinking.

- Don't be surprised if the question you perceive to be completely harmless seems to horrify your loved one. The less you have talked with each other, the more likely you will stumble onto something that seems innocent enough to you but is packed with emotion for your loved one. The photograph of the sour-faced woman you never knew might be the grandmother who delighted in telling your mother when she was a young girl that she would never find a husband if she didn't lose weight. You can't always know which question will strike a nerve. When it does, simply set that question aside. In the beginning, you might have to focus more on establishing a comfortable dialogue with your loved ones rather than on receiving a substantive response to your question. As your loved ones become more comfortable with you in the role of questioner, they will be able to give increasingly thoughtful and meaningful answers.

Just as your legacy, the gift of you, is yours to define and to offer unconditionally to those you choose, you can also ask your loved ones to give that same gift to you. "Ask and you shall receive" might not be your reward today, tomorrow, next month, next year, or ever. But if a loved one isn't talking and you don't take a risk by asking, you, like so many people I interviewed, will have to continue to live with your "oh wells." If you don't initiate the conversation with someone who is unable to do so, the essence of his or her life might always remain a mystery to you. Don't let that happen. Who knows, when you try, you just might discover it's yours for the asking!

✺ 10 ✺

Final Thoughts

At that time, everybody was good to one another. People needed each other so much. People don't need each other anymore. There's not that connection. My kids don't seem to feel it at all.

—Helen, seventy-one-year-old mother and grandmother

Helen was fourteen years old, living on the family farm outside of a small village near Munich during World War II. The only people left in her village at the end of the war were "women, old men, and very young boys." All able-bodied men and teenage boys were conscripted into the German army for a final stand against the approaching Allied forces. Helen vividly described the bombing raids that destroyed the nearby village. This is the story she told:

We would be playing outside like children do. Then we would start hearing the awful noise that the planes made as they got closer and closer. There were maybe fifty to a hundred planes at a time. They flew so low, I could see the faces of the pilots. I'm not kidding you. It was so frightening. I would stand there and watch them fly right over me. There was a munition plant in the village that they were after. . . . My father had dug a bomb shelter next to our house. We would stay in the shelter until the bombing stopped. Once in a while a bomb would hit close to where we lived, so we hid in the shelter just in case. Then, I would have to go with the other teenage girls into the village to look for bodies. We were assigned by the local authorities to pull bodies out of the rubble of the bombed-out buildings. You see, there was no one else left to do it."

Helen, only a ninth grader, who was just starting to become interested in boys, on one day would be doing the things that typical fourteen-year-old girls do, and on the next day would be climbing through smoldering piles of bricks looking for the dead and dying.

But Helen doesn't only tell stories about the horrors of the war. She fondly remembers that it was also a time when "people needed each other so much." People were connected with each other. They comforted each other. They shared their food. They relied on each other for survival. As Helen said, "We had a feeling of closeness then, that I don't feel today with my own family. We take so much for granted today. Back then, you didn't know if you would be alive the next day. So, I think you appreciated each other and what you had."

On September 11, 2001, over three thousand people died in the attacks on the World Trade Center and the Pentagon. These horrific acts stunned our nation. We felt vulnerable in a way we had not experienced since the attack on Pearl Harbor sixty years earlier. We worried about the safety of our loved ones and ourselves.

How did we react to the attacks? Just like Helen and her family did during World War II. We turned to each other for comfort, solace, and reassurance. Less than a month after the terrorist attacks, a Time/CNN poll reported that Americans felt a renewed commitment to "values related to family." Six out of ten people said they felt a need to spend more time with family members. In the wake of the devastation, two-thirds of the people polled had told family members they loved them. More than half felt they had "a greater focus in life." Suddenly, we felt much closer to and much more in need of the people we love.

The Evolution of the Generations

Wars, national tragedies, and personal crises have a history of awakening our emotions and stirring our souls. They make us reach out to our loved ones. We talk more with them. We spend more time with them. We start to come down our ladders.

But, eventually, each crisis passes. We go back to our old ways. Back up our ladders. Back to our own private thoughts and our own worlds. Do we have to suffer through a personal tragedy or national devastation in order to awaken ourselves to what is important in our lives? Are we capable of sustaining the initial burst of intimacy with our loved ones after the crisis has passed? Is it simply in our nature to climb right back up our ladders when we no longer feel the immediate need to give or receive reassurance and comfort?

We can learn how to keep connected to our loved ones and how to stay off our ladders if we commit ourselves to identifying the What and Why of our lives and then to consciously and purposely giving them to the people we love. For most of us, talking about ourselves does not happen naturally. We not only have to learn how to give the gift of ourselves, we first have to identify what really does matter to us and why we live the way we do. When we do that self-examination and share the outcome with the people we love, giving the gift of ourselves can become a natural part of everyday life, just like brushing our teeth in the morning, driving the same way to work each day, or casually exchanging an "I love you" with someone we care about.

But it does take practice. Especially for those of us who were raised in families in which people shared living space with each other but not the essence of their lives. My interviews revealed that members of my generation, the baby boomers, seem more emotionally ready than our parents were to begin a dialogue about ourselves with our children. I also found that Generation Xers seem even more willing to open their lives to the people they love than we baby boomers are. Don, a thirty-six-year-old father of three, gives a glimpse of the evolution of the generations toward more emotional openness and self-disclosure:

My grandfather was a pretty hard-bitten farmer, embittered about a lot of things that happened to him. You weren't meant to enjoy life. You were meant to get through it. So coming out of that background, my dad was not going to be emotionally what he might have been otherwise. But he has built on the prior generation. I remember the first time—I was in college—that we greeted each other with a hug. I'm sure that was a big step for him because it was not a natural part of his upbringing. Now, he even tells me that he loves me.

Don recognizes that his dad's ability to express his emotions is limited by his upbringing. But Don also knows that his father has made emotional progress beyond the generation that raised him. As Don said about his dad, "He has built on the prior generation." Don has in turn built on his dad's generation. He makes time for his own children, two girls ages twelve and ten, and an eight-year-old son. He reads bedtime stories to them. He has conversations with them when they are eating meals together. He is much more open and emotionally available for his children than his dad was for him.

The World War II generation, which Tom Brokaw described as "The Greatest Generation" in his bestselling book of the same name, is indeed a special group of people. They made incredible personal sacrifices. They were tested in ways that we, their offspring, cannot relate to at all. They endured a national depression and fought a global war.

They worry that their children and grandchildren might not possess the toughness to withstand hard times. Byron calls them a "soft generation." He wonders if "we did have another war, would they be willing to fight?" Louise thinks that for the younger generation, "self-fulfillment comes first." Marge worries that her children indulge her grandchildren's "every whim." But along with concerns that the younger generations are excessively self-absorbed and self-indulgent, their parents and grandparents marvel at how emotionally available they are for their children. They too see the evolution of the generations:

> My daughter does a really good job of explaining things to her daughter, much better than I did with her.
>
> —Martha, age seventy-one

> The kids will tease their mom and joke with her. I wouldn't think of doing that with my mother.   —Leonard, age sixty-nine

> Today, our children and grandchildren talk to each other. They explain how they feel about things. We couldn't . . . I couldn't do that with my parents.   —Daphne, age sixty-two

> My son doesn't tolerate any nonsense, but he also does a lot more hugging and talking with his two boys than I did with

him and his sister. I'm a little surprised by it. I never pictured him in the role of a father. [laughs] He's a good dad.

—Evelyn, age seventy-four

As we consciously bring the What and Why of our lives down the ladder, not only do our children directly benefit from knowing us in a more meaningful way, they also learn how to interact in the same healthy manner with their off-spring. And as we build on what our parent's generation was able to tell us about themselves, our children's generation will be able to build on what we were able to share with them.

My interview with Troy shows that we might indeed be heading in the right direction. I asked Troy, a thirty-seven-year-old father of two boys ages twelve and nine, to speculate about what one thing he had done with his children that they would always remember. Without hesitation he said, "That's a great question. Let me get them on the phone right now and ask them." He called home and talked to each boy on the speakerphone from his office. He asked them the same question I posed to him. Both boys gave essentially the same answer: "Going down the giant slides at Water World, Dad!" His older son added: "The best part was watching you do those belly flops, Dad!" Troy smiled and said, "You two just like seeing an old guy like me with a big belly act like a little kid." Both boys laughed out loud. I was struck by Troy's openness with the boys and theirs with him. No one hesitated to say what he felt even with me listening to the conversation.

I was unable to have that kind of spontaneous interaction with my dad. It's a simple but powerful example of one generation building on the next. And the building process will accelerate as we become more proficient at channeling the emotional openness of today's world into a purposeful transfer of the What and Why of our lives to our loved ones.

Don't Wallow in the Past, Learn from It

Let's begin with the parents, and let's begin with some common sense.

Wipe it out. Zero. Nada.

"But," you say, "they blah, blah, blah, blah."

So what? In the first place, maybe they weren't as bad as you think, but so what? Maybe they were just downright cruel, selfish, unreasonable schmucks, but the question remains, so what? . . .

> But if you start probing into the past, whining about all
> your grievances and bad memories, there's no end to it. Will
> you be healed? Never. You will just wallow in victimization.
> —Bill O'Reilly, *The O'Reilly Factor*

Before this book ends, let's make sure one thing is perfectly clear. I am not suggesting that you or I should use the limitations of our parents as an excuse for our own faults and failings. But with that said, I will see my dad on his ladder until the day I die. I will always live with the sadness of never really knowing who he was. This has had a profound effect on how I lived my life. I learned many wonderful lessons in life from watching my dad. I learned how to work hard, how to provide for a family, and how to live a good and decent life. But I also learned that it was okay to spend my life at the top of a ladder while my loved ones stood at the bottom. I learned that it was okay to live in my own private world while they were left wondering who I was and what I was really thinking about.

Do I blame my father for teaching me this? Or my mother for letting it happen?

No. Am I willing to look at it honestly, recognize the damage it did, and try to give a better legacy to my children? Absolutely.

Whine about the past? Don't waste your time. Wallow in it? You're better than that. But say "So what?" as Mr. O'Reilly and many other commentators on American life recommend, when looking at the faults and failures of your parents? What a terrible waste of an opportunity to make life better for you and the people you love. "Probing into the past," as Mr. O'Reilly calls it, does not necessarily mean looking for someone to blame for the problems in your life. It can and should mean that you are willing to face your past and learn from it, so you don't perpetuate the same mistakes with your children. I believe that's exactly what my mother and father would want me to do. They would want me to make a better life for my children, just as they tried to do for me.

So, get eyeball-to-eyeball with your past. See it for what it was, understand what it did and didn't give you, and above all else, learn from it. By doing so, you don't blame your parents, you honor them. Build on whatever your parents gave you. Give the gift of yourself to your loved ones, even if your parents never gave it to you. And start asking for that same gift from those who have never shared the What and Why of their lives with you. Set the standard for openness and intimacy among your loved ones. Be the first generation in your family to initiate a purposeful sharing of the What and Why of your life with the people you love. What a wonderful legacy to begin giving, a legacy that can be a part of the fabric of your family for generations to come!